Love Lift Me Higher

Love Lift Me Higher

Meditations on Finding True Happiness

by

Dorothy Marcic

George Ronald
Oxford

George Ronald, *Publisher*
Oxford
www.grbooks.com

Reprinted 2011

*A catalogue record for this book is available
from the British Library*

ISBN 978–0–85398–539–6

Cover design: Steiner Graphics

Contents

To my mother,
Leone Stordock Evert,
whose love is my foundation

Introduction

Bestow upon me a heart which, like unto a glass,
may be illumined with the light of Thy love,
and confer upon me thoughts which may change
this world into a rose garden through the outpourings
of heavenly grace.
'Abdu'l-Bahá[1]

Recent social science research indicates that 30 minutes a day spent reading or mediating about love can dramatically impact a person's level of happiness and those effects can be seen within two weeks. Why not, then, read short quotations and stories daily, in order to be happier? What could be easier?

This book offers such quotations and stories, as well as exercises and worksheets, on a number of themes. The organization of the book allows the reader to start at any chapter, making it simple to read short sections at a time.

The book is divided into chapters representing different aspects of love and other virtues, with quotations designed to touch hearts and give tools to solve daily problems in one's relationships, families, at work and with the Creator. Some topics explore love in relationship to other virtues. For example, love without trustworthiness is hollow and love without justice can become oppression. Each chapter comprises not only stories from various people, describing how love positively impacted, and perhaps even changed, their lives, but also contains exercises designed to help you figure out how to apply these wonderful, but sometimes mysterious, concepts and principles.

You may choose to go through the exercises alone or you can do them in a group. If you work with others, the process is to fill out the table alone and then answer the questions as a group. Appoint someone as a facilitator and ask that person to make sure there is participation from all members.

My hope is that in these pages you will find solace, understanding and, yes, even happiness.

Dr Dorothy Marcic
www.drdorothy.com
dorothy@marcic.com
August 2009

Preface

Even before positive psychology was identified as a field, it appealed to me. From the publication of Martin Seligman's *Learned Optimism*, I was hooked. The idea you could study behaviors such as learned helplessness and scientifically understand the dynamics was liberating. By the time that book came out in 1992, I had already been giving presentations and seminars for 15 years on personal motivation, overcoming inner obstacles and learning to create more fulfilling relationships, both at home and at work. I was primed for positive psychology.

Then, a couple of years ago, I had a moment of clarity. All the results of the myriad studies were really quantifying the wisdom of the ages, as taught to us through the holy books of various religions. So research shows people who are grateful and forgiving are happier and healthier? Oh, that's why the world's religions exhort us to have gratitude and to forgive others. Here is one place science is actually catching up with religion, thanks to positive psychology.

When Seligman gave the field its title at a talk in 1998, a lot of us took note and rallied around. To be sure, the term 'positive psychology' was coined by the master himself, Abraham Maslow (in *Motivation and Personality*), while other psychologists had also written on themes of love and happiness. Erich Fromm (*The Art of Loving*) had been all the rage when I was in college, and when I was in graduate school I discovered Carl Rogers, the father of non-directive interviewing and one of the first to recognize the power of authentic communication. Two lesser-known researchers who touched me deeply were Mary Parker Follett and Fritz Roethlisberger.

Mary Parker Follett wrote about the necessity of workers belonging to a group or team. Trouble was, these articles came out in the 1920s and, aside from the fact that women were not taken seriously, people thought her ideas too 'communist'. Finally, the world caught up with her and her works were republished in 1995 (see *Mary Parker Follett: Prophet of Management*).

When I came across Fritz Roethlisberger, as a result of long discussions with colleague Peter Vaill, I was entranced. Roethlisberger was one of the original researchers on the late 1920s General Electric plant Hawthorne Studies, which discovered that people at work need to feel the belongingness of a group. Roethlisberger (see *Management and the Worker*) became a tireless advocate for workplace community. Some of his ideas can be seen later in Jerry Harvey's work, most notably *How Come Every Time I Get Stabbed in the Back My Fingerprints are on the Knife?* Peter Vaill's work on love and spirit (see *Spirited Leading and Learning: Process Wisdom for a New Age*) also owes a great deal to Roethlisberger. My own book on *Managing with the Wisdom of Love* is also built on the legacy of these thought leaders.

When I conceived the idea to write this new book I saw it as a way to help people become happier, as a way for them to find skills to have more fulfilling lives, to learn to love more completely, and to do so by understanding how religion and spirituality have given us the prescription all along. Now the science of psychology has affirmed those 'spiritual laws', many of which go back to ancient times. No matter how much we use Facebook, Twitter, LinkedIn, text messages or plain old face-to-face, no matter how many spreadsheets we need for the vitality of our enterprises, no matter how many virtual meetings we attend, it is the love, engagement and connection that keep us going, that restore our hearts and souls.

Acknowledgements

Every book builds not only on previous thinkers but also on the intellectual and emotional support of a myriad people. No woman is an island, and certainly not when writing a manuscript. Gratitude, therefore, should be nearly infinite but I will do my best to contain it in these pages.

First I must thank Shahriar Razavi. As I sat in his office at the Bahá'í World Centre a couple of years ago in Haifa, Israel, he lovingly encouraged me to write another book. At the time I was deeply involved in my new profession of playwriting and was not very keen on this idea. But a few months later, as I was watching a documentary on 'Happiness', an idea popped into my head and here you see the result. Razavi's suggestion helped me be ready when the concept struck. One of Razavi's colleagues, Stephen Birkland, has refreshed and reassured me at so many junctures, I lose count. Next, I could not have done this without Wendi Momen of George Ronald, who immediately saw the power of the theme and who capably edited throughout the entire process. May Hofman of George Ronald was also a continuing beacon of light. Other idea champions include Bob and Debbie Rosenfeld, long-time friends and colleagues; Edris Taborn, who invited me to present the book's concepts at Louhelen Bahá'í School, which really helped me see what worked; Brian Kurzius, whose books *Fire and Gold* and *Hidden Gifts* have been the source of deep solace, and whose generosity of spirit brightened my soul; Georgia Sauer, writer extraordinaire, who is always upbeat about my projects; Lynn Lobban, who warmly included me in a wonderful writers' group; Kathleen McEnerny, whose academic insights are always meaningful; Richard L. Oliver, whose spiritual quest and questions have helped me gain deeper understandings; Larry Miller, whose prolific writing continues to be a source of inspiration; Karen Streets-Anderson, whose long and intellectual discussions are always a salve to my mind and spirit; Xerox that same thought for her uncle, Donald Streets; Jane Faily, whose integration of the intellectual and spiritual has always left me in a state of awe; Mary K. Radpour, whose insights into psychology and spirituality have had a profound impact on me; Mehr Mansuri, a friend and colleague who helps challenge my thinking in so many ways; John Didonna, whose competence and ability to garner resources always astounds me; Andi Seals, whose own spiritual growth through suffering has taught me much; Gary Hogenson, whose love and prayers are always, always there; Douglas and Suzanne Henck, whose selfless service is a beacon of light; Carolyn Stalcup, whose friendship and graphic design skills have kept me afloat on many occasions; Susan Stengel, my friend since college, someone who has ended up working in similar cities over the years; Bambi Betts, who always provides intellectual and soulful connection; David Friendlander, the theatrical attorney from heaven; Judi Neal, long an advocate of applying spiritual values; Homa Tavangar, who was supportive while in the throes of her own book-writing; Ruha Reyhani, who helped me learn to tweet; Sharon Hurt, whose own dignity under difficulties has been a role model; Peter Vaill, whose long-time friendship has informed much of my thinking; producers Bill Franzblau and Jamie Cesa, whose continuous support of my writing has kept me going through some long and winding roads; Hinton Battle, whose creativity takes my breath away; and some recent writing teachers who have brought me to a new level: Marsha Norman, Karen Hartman and Jeffrey Sweet. Many friends continue to rally around my efforts, writing and otherwise: Faran and Tali Ferdowsi, Lishy Price, Nikki Gundry, Joel Rothstein, Fruz and Amir Roshan-Far, Alison and Parker McGee, Zana Ziegler, Ellie Jacobi, Carol Caldwell, Kathy Diaz, Shannon Hecht, Kathryn Runde, Roberta Law, Ziba and Farzin Ferdowsi, Joan Gallos, Gordon Naylor, Maxine and Mark Rossman, Jeremy and Tahirih Naylor Thimm, Joan Weiner, Joe Seltzer, Mark Cannon, Sandy Toson, Stella Reed, Lana Bogan, Leslie and Kurt Asplund, Marie Volpe, Peter Neaman and Victoria Marsick, George Starcher, Daniel Truran, Cecelia Harel, Walter Ezell, Monte Hanson, Cherie Chakiban, Hillary Chapman, David Hall, Daniel Truran, Laura D'Angelo, Bill and Vahideh Ahlhauser, Amy Lynch, Aram and Farsheed Ferdowsi, Matty Thimm, Diti and Bill Geissler, Franz Grebacher, Jane Hardy, Muna Alhilli, Holly Tashian, Carolyn Oehler, Penny Frere, Kacky Fell, Tara McDougal, Barbara Sanders, Barbara Moss, Sharon Carr, Eileen Norman, Lysa Parker, Barbara Nicholson, Linda Assaf and Mina Sabet Bogan. For theatrical upliftment in Nashville: Maryanna and Chris Clark, Kimberley LaMarque, Wesley Paine and Trish Crist. I cannot finish these gratitudes without mentioning my two assistants, Allison Greer in Nashville and Thomas Higgins in New York. Both of them are so smart all I have to do some days is just get out of their way. And they are thoughtful, sincere, focused and hard-working. How blessed that I have them in my life! Because Allison has worked for me so long, she has also become a friend and a comforting work companion. And there are so many more wonderful friends who have helped. I love you all!

Finally, I could never be where I am without the love and encouragement of my family: my husband Richard, whose own knowledge of writing has been a continuous fount of learning; my brother-in-law, Iskandar Hai, whose mastery of religious texts has taught me a great deal; Hami and Attusa Hai, whose love and hospitality is a joy to behold; my step-daughters Amy Summers and Danielle Legg; my sister Janet Mittelsteadt and her husband, Dick, who keep me grounded, remembering my roots in small-town Wisconsin; and my three daughters, Roxanne, who helped in the early days with quotation-researching; Solange, whose Quito wedding to the marvellous Carlos during the whole process of this book was a most uplifting experience; and Elizabeth, who just graduated from college in music and is now happily a math teacher. From my family I have learned what love is, how imperfect we often are in its delivery, and how to mend and improve what was hurt. We know our own love largely through its reflection back from others.

1 Choose Love

But now faith, hope, love, abide these three;
but the greatest of these is love.
I Corinthians 13:13

Love has such a wonderful sound to it. It's uplifting to think about it, hope for it; but when it's gone, the loss is mourned. The problem is, we spend way more time thinking about love coming to us rather than about the love we give to others. And yet, giving love is the very dynamic that brings us the most joy and inner contentment. The old saying, 'It is better to give than to receive' isn't just an empty slogan. It really is better. Research has shown over and over that people who give to others are happier. What I hope this book gets across is: 1) You can choose to give more love and 2) science and research can help us understand love more thoroughly. Though love is an emotion, you can use your mind, your intellect, to decide that love will be a more potent force in your life, even if just a little more each day. 'Let each morn be better than its eve and each morrow richer than its yesterday.'[1] Like many other people, I struggle with conceptions of love, how much is enough or too much, putting an effort into choosing love rather than waiting for it to fall on me, transcending resentment and envies, and breaking down defenses that keep me from loving others.

Desire to love

Beloved, if God so loved us, we ought also to love one another.[2]

Create in me a pure heart, O my God, and renew a tranquil conscience within me, O my Hope![3]

Through the power of Thy transcendent might lift me up unto the heaven of Thy holiness, O Source of my being . . .[4]

Possess a pure, kindly and radiant heart, that thine may be a sovereignty ancient, imperishable and everlasting.[5]

In the garden of thy heart plant naught but the rose of love . . .[6]

Hatred stirreth up strifes: but love covereth all sins.[7]

We must be united. We must love each other. We must ever praise each other.[8]

He that loveth not knoweth not God; for God is love.[9]

Love is a powerful force

Your great love refreshes me.[10]

In the world of existence there is no more powerful magnet than the magnet of love.[11]

For hate is never conquered by hate.
Hate is conquered by love.
This is an eternal law.[12]

Bestow upon me a heart which, like unto a glass, may be illumined with the light of Thy love, and confer upon me thoughts which may change this world into a rose garden through the outpouring of heavenly grace.[13]

What a power is love! It is the most wonderful, the greatest of all living powers.
     Love gives life to the lifeless. Love lights a flame in the heart that is cold. Love brings hope to the hopeless and gladdens the hearts of the sorrowful.[14]

Thou shalt love thy neighbor as thyself.[15]

Science and love

I hope that thou wilt progress more and more; that thou wilt increase thy knowledge and science; and that thou wilt ever strive for gentleness and love.[16]

. . . the foundation of the law of God [is] the acquisition of divine virtues, morality, love, the development of arts and sciences and the spirit of the oneness of humanity.[17]

Strive towards love

Let brotherly love continue.[18]

Undisturbed shall our mind remain, no evil words shall escape our lips; friendly and full of sympathy shall we remain, with heart full of love, and free from any hidden malice; and that person shall we penetrate with loving thoughts, wide, deep, boundless, freed from anger and hatred.[19]

Be kind to all around and serve one another; love to be just and true in all your dealings; pray always and so live your life that sorrow cannot touch you.[20]

Strive always that you may be united. Kindness and love in the path of service must be your means.[21]

All God's prophets have brought the message of love. None has ever thought that war and hate are good. Every one agrees in saying that love and kindness are best.[22]

A new commandment I give unto you, That ye love one another; as I have loved you, that ye also love one another.[23]

Love requires action

Love manifests its reality in deeds, not only in words – these alone are without effect. In order that love may manifest its power there must be an object, an instrument, a motive.[24]

If I love you, I need not continually speak of my love – you will know without any words.[25]

. . . the way to broaden the outlook of the very narrow-hearted and prejudiced, and to make them listen to a wider teaching, was by showing towards them the greatest kindness and love.[26]

Be always kind to everyone and a refuge for those who are without shelter.
Be daughters to those who are older than you.
Be sisters to those who are of your own age.
Be mothers to those who are younger than yourselves.
Be nurses to the sick, treasurers for the poor, and supply heavenly food to the hungry.[27]

Ye are the fruits of one tree, and the leaves of one branch. Deal ye one with another with the utmost love and harmony, with friendliness and fellowship . . . So powerful is the light of unity that it can illuminate the whole earth.[28]

Let us be united and love one another and await the result. We know the effects of war are bad. So let us try, as an experiment, peace, and if the results of peace are bad, then we can choose if it would be better to go back to the old state of war! Let us in any case make the experiment. If we see that unity brings Light we shall continue it.[29]

Sincerity and love will conquer hate.[30]

When a thought of war comes, oppose it by a stronger thought of peace. A thought of hatred must be destroyed by a more powerful thought of love. Thoughts of war bring destruction to all harmony, well-being, restfulness and content.[31]

. . . the radiance of the world is due to love; the well-being and happiness of the world depend upon it. Therefore, I admonish you that you must strive throughout the human world to diffuse the light of love.[32]

Lack of love can hurt

> If we are caused joy or pain by a friend, if a love prove true or false, it is the soul that is affected. If our dear ones are far from us – it is the soul that grieves, and the grief or trouble of the soul may react on the body.[33]

> When we find truth, constancy, fidelity, and love, we are happy; but if we meet with lying, faithlessness, and deceit, we are miserable.[34]

> In short, whatsoever thing is arranged in harmony and with love and purity of motive, its result is light, and should the least trace of estrangement prevail the result shall be darkness upon darkness . . .[35]

Exercise

Think of several people with whom you want to have a more positive relationship, in other words, with whom you would like more love, more positive emotion. Fill in the table on page 6.

Questions to ask yourself

1) What has been keeping me from making these relationships more positive?

2) Do I you see any patterns in the dynamics of the different relationships?

3) How easy or difficult will it be for me to implement the steps I've laid out? Can I get support from others to make sure I do these things?

Having better relationships

Name of person with whom I want a better relationship	Describe current relationship	What would I rather have in the relationship?	What steps can I take to make the relationship more positive?
1)			
2)			
3)			
4)			

Blocks to love

If love is so wonderful, fills us with such bliss, why aren't we giving it, sharing it at every possible nanosecond? Sometimes it is fear of rejection, anger at past hurts or just plain awkwardness. Often, though, it is our own ego, our own 'insistent self',[36] that keeps us from loving others. That insistent self becomes our alter ego, convincing us that we are too important, that others deserve less, that they should take care of us and not the other way around, etc. I've noticed in myself that if I am totally convinced of my position and resist even listening to others, then I know the insistent self has its grip on me: 'the insistent self, the evil promptings of the human heart'.[37] Our egos keep us attached to material objects or material aspects of another person (such as looks, clothing or sexual attraction). Real love transcends the material world. It is essentially spiritual in nature. But our ego wants us to keep focused on the material world, on our material desires, on the hurts and wounds we've felt subjected to.

No man can be made happy by wealth.[38]

There are two contrasting forces working within man, the animal nature and the spiritual one. Self and passion may be described as the expression of the animal nature . . . which tends to drag him down into the abyss of material existence. On the other hand, the soul, which emanates from the spiritual worlds of God, becomes, if illumined with the light of faith, the motive power for the elevation . . . into the realms of the spirit.[39]

If . . . pride and vainglory . . . dominate . . . man will become a prisoner of his own self and passion.[40]

Free thyself from the fetters of this world, and loose thy soul from the prison of self.[41]

When one is released from the prison of self, that is indeed release, for that is the greater prison.[42]

Exercise

Complete the sentences below. Be as honest as you can and write down what comes first to your mind, as that is usually what you really feel. If you think about it a while and then write, you are more likely to write down what you think you *should* feel. So put down your first thoughts.

1) I get really annoyed when someone . . .

2) I am happiest when a person . . .

3) I wish people were more . . .

4) I lose patience if a person . . .

5) It is really fun to be around people when . . .

6) One thing I would change about myself is how I react when . . .

7) I feel superior to others when . . .

8) I feel inferior, or humbler, than others when . . .

9) The best connections I have with others are . . .

Questions

1) Can you see some patterns in what you like and dislike in others?

2) Have you ever tried to change another person? A spouse/partner, child, etc? How successful were you?

3) How do your expectations of others get in the way of positive relationships?

4) What can you do to increase your positive interactions with others?

When there are unresolved and chronic conflicts with others, especially those involving long-term work colleagues or personal relationships, you have the choice of either a) getting angry and annoyed because the other person does not behave in the way you think is correct; or b) accepting the person 'as is' and working around his or her personality (this does not include situations of violence or abuse, where remedying the situation – often by getting out – is demanded). High stress is often related to being unable to accept others and a continual nagging or unspoken expectation for the other person to be otherwise. This is rarely successful. If you are able, look at yourself and ask: What is it about me that is having a problem with this person? What is inside me that triggers someone else's behavior? Answering such questions is a lifelong exercise and one gets better at it as time goes on. When I taught seminars on 'Dealing with Difficult People', I discovered the worst problem for people in these situations was their reaction to the difficult person. No matter where you go, what job you have, what volunteer opportunity, there will always be difficult, demanding people. If you spend your life looking for an idyllic spot without them, you'll be on a fool's quest. Anyone who's been married knows how hard it is to change another person. The only hope is to change yourself and how you react to the unruly individual. In that way, also, you grow.

. . . your own difficulties . . . are the means of your spirit growing and developing. You will suddenly find that you have conquered many of the problems which upset you, and then you will wonder why they should have troubled you at all.[43]

Story: Love was the only choice

The last year of my mother's life was tough on all of us: my brother, me, but mostly our mom. She had Alzheimer's and was in and out of normal consciousness, sometimes remembering us, sometimes not. Then there was her paranoia, imagining people were taking things from her, or trying to harm her. After trying so many things, I came to realize the only thing that 'worked' was pure love. You might say I chose to love, but really, there was nothing else that helped. Just sitting with her, smiling, listening to her senseless talk, reassuring her fears, agreeing with her indignations.

In February we had to move her from assisted living to a nursing home. As I arrived for the first time, she ran up to me, throwing her arms around me and shouting, 'You are my savior. You've got to get me out of here.' Their offense? Not giving her salt and pepper shakers and ketchup at dinner. To be fair to my mother, her room wasn't great and the staff seemed coolly distant. Luckily we found her another nursing home where they knew how to care for her with patience and concern. She got her own salt and pepper and ketchup. That didn't mean she lost her paranoia. When I visited I heard her warnings about how they had stolen her purse (the nurses put it away for safekeeping), about the people who were coming into her room at night to mess it up, about the other patients who were gossiping about her or trying to knock her down. All I could do was listen intently, nodding my head, assenting to her wild ideas.

But I came to see it didn't matter. All that mattered was that I was there with her, really *with* her, and that seemed to offer her comfort at times. Over those many months I began to see it calmed me too, gave me reassurance that the woman who had borne me was spending her last days as well as she could. I gradually learned to let go of all the things that I wanted to do, wanted to change. I accepted the inevitable evidence that I could produce no change, at least in material circumstances. Instead, eventually I surrendered to the quiet, expansive sufficiency of love, and love saved us both. One day my mother died and she died well. She had lunch, got up and dropped dead to the ground. It was reported she thought it was a good lunch. My mother always appreciated good food. Just one of the things I still love about her most dearly.

Robert Zangler, Physical Therapist
Franklin, Tennessee

2 Love and Happiness

All the great thinkers and religious leaders say happiness comes from within, not from possessions or status. Yet we live in a time of great acquisition, where well-being is pursued through a bigger house, faster car, more elegant clothing, prestigious jobs and friends. Recent worldwide research on happiness[1] indicates it can be attained through the following: close relationships, meaningful work,[2] service, a sense of purpose (which can derive from relationships, service and work) and hope, and being involved in something greater than oneself. The pursuit of happiness through material gratification just doesn't work. Happiness is more about where you are going and whom you love.

> The grand essentials of happiness are: something to do, something to love, and something to hope for. *Allan K. Chalmers*

Love brings happiness

> Thoughts of love are constructive of brotherhood, peace, friendship, and happiness.[3]

> Lift up your self by yourself;
> examine your self by yourself.
> Thus self-protected and attentive
> you will live joyfully, mendicant.
> For self is the master of self . . .[4]

> The greatest gift of man is universal love – that magnet which renders existence eternal. It attracts realities and diffuses life with infinite joy. If this love penetrate the heart of man, all the forces of the universe will be realized in him . . . Strive to . . . make your

hearts greater centers of attraction and to create new ideals and relationships.[5]

. . . the wise man who takes pleasure in giving is thereby happy hereafter.[6]

Exercise

The scales on page 14 relate to the elements of happiness. Rank yourself from 1 to 10 on each of them. A score of 1 is low while 10 is high. Next, describe where you are, what you do for each item. For example, write down which close relationships you have (or don't have), the nature of your meaningful work or lack thereof, etc. Finally, list ideas you have for becoming better under each of the six elements of happiness.

Questions

1) How similar or different is this definition of happiness from what you thought before? How do you think others define happiness?

2) In which elements are you strongest? Weakest? Do you have any reasons why some are stronger for you?

3) What will you do this week to become happier?

Contentment brings happiness

Grieve not at the divine trials. Be not troubled because of hardships and ordeals; turn unto God, bowing in humbleness and praying to Him, while bearing every ordeal, contented under all conditions and thankful in every difficulty.[7]

. . . be firm and steadfast, for by it man attains the greatest hope. Bear

Elements of happiness

	Rate yourself 1–10 (10 is highest)	Describe what you do for each item	How can you improve?
Close relationships			
Meaningful work			
Service			
A sense of purpose			
Hope			
Being involved in something greater than yourself			

every difficulty and be content with any ordeal for the love of thy Lord
...[8]

Meditation and happiness

According to Jonathan Haidt, your level of happiness can be easily increased in any of these three ways: meditation, cognitive therapy or using Prozac.

> Though one were to live a hundred years without wisdom and with a mind unstilled by meditation, the life of a single day is better if one is wise and practices meditation.[9]

> Through the faculty of meditation man attains to eternal life; through it he receives the breath of the Holy Spirit – the bestowal of the Spirit is given in reflection and meditation.

> The spirit of man is itself informed and strengthened during meditation; through it affairs of which man knew nothing are unfolded before his view. Through it he receives Divine inspiration, through it he receives heavenly food.[10]

> There is no meditation without wisdom, and there is no wisdom without meditation. When a man has both meditation and wisdom, he is indeed close to nirvana.[11]

Love and happiness affect both body and spirit

> Love is the means of the most great happiness in both the material and spiritual worlds![12]

> Happiness consists of two kinds: physical and spiritual. The physical happiness is limited; its utmost duration is one day, one month, one year. It hath no result. Spiritual happiness is eternal and unfathomable. This kind of happiness appeareth in one's soul with the love of God and suffereth one to attain to the virtues and perfections of the world of humanity. Therefore, endeavor as much as thou art able in order to illuminate the lamp of thy heart by the light of love.[13]

Happiness is a great healer to those who are ill.[14]

Work can be more meaningful and more fulfilling when it is successful, which requires focus of thought and energy and is much helped when we love what we do.

> So long as the thoughts of an individual are scattered he will achieve no results, but if his thinking be concentrated on a single point wonderful will be the fruits thereof.
> One cannot obtain the full force of the sunlight when it is cast on a flat mirror, but once the sun shineth upon a concave mirror, or on a lens that is convex, all its heat will be concentrated on a single point, and that one point will burn the hottest. Thus is it necessary to focus one's thinking on a single point so that it will become an effective force.[15]

> Nothing is too much trouble when one loves, and there is always time.[16]

Exercise

Think of your typical week, all the things you do for home, for family, for your religion, for friends and community. Complete the table on page 17. You are asked to assign a percentage of your time spent on different types of activities – you can make very rough estimates:

1)   Things you *must* do. This includes pay your rent or mortgage, go to work, get your kids ready for school, etc.

2)   Things you *should* do, which might include such tasks as going to a company event in the evening, volunteering at your child's school, voting, cleaning your house or car, preparing nutritious meals, etc.

3)   Things you *like* to do, which might include going to the movies, cooking, socializing, meditating, watching television, etc.

4) Things you *love* to do. These are activities that energize you, make you feel alive and fulfilled and can be for work or not.

Things I do	Percentage of my time spent	What are the types of activities?
Things I *must* do		
Things I *should* do		
Things I *like* to do		
Things I *love* to do		
Total per cent	100	

Everyone has a certain number of *musts* and *shoulds* but if you find yourself spending most of your time on those two, you likely are feeling burned out much of the time. If you can, over time, increase the percentage of *likes* and *loves*, you will have more energy and enthusiasm. Even when you volunteer, choose activities that interest you, whenever you can. You will generally give better service and you will also be happier. Everybody wins.

Questions

1) Are you surprised at the amount of time you spend on *shoulds*?

2) What are some concrete things you can do to increase the time spent on *likes* and *loves*?

3) What keeps you from doing the things in number 2?

4)   How can you encourage others to spend more time on *likes* and *loves*?

Bring happiness to others

The doer of good rejoices both ways. He rejoices at the thought, 'I have done good', and rejoices even more when he comes to a happy state.[17]

Let all your striving be for this, to become the source of life and immortality, and peace and comfort and joy, to every human soul, whether one known to you or a stranger, one opposed to you or on your side.[18]

Be ye salutary water to every thirsty one, a wise guide to every one led astray, an affectionate father or mother to every orphan, and, in the utmost joy and fragrance, a son or daughter to every one bent with age.[19]

If you attain to such a capacity of love and unity, [He] will shower infinite graces of the spiritual Kingdom upon you, guide, protect and preserve you under the shadow of His Word, increase your happiness in this world and uphold you through all difficulties.[20]

Be as a lamp unto them that walk in darkness, a joy to the sorrowful, a sea for the thirsty, a haven for the distressed, an upholder and defender of the victim of oppression.[21]

May all of you become the cause of joy and of renewing the fire of the love of God in all hearts.[22]

. . . be ye compassionate and kind to all the human race. Deal ye with strangers the same as with friends, cherish ye others just as ye would your own. See foes as friends; see demons as angels . . .[23]

. . . bring ye rest and peace to the disturbed; make ye a provision for the destitute; be a treasury of riches for the poor; be a healing medicine for those who suffer pain; be ye doctor and nurse to the ailing; promote ye friendship, and honor, and conciliation . . .[24]

. . . you must love and cherish each individual member of humanity.[25]

'Work,' he said unceasingly, 'for the day of Universal Peace. Strive always that you may be united. Kindness and love in the path of service must be your means.'[26]

. . . the wise man who takes pleasure in giving is thereby happy hereafter.[27]

Exercise

Using the chart on page 20, think of four people you can make happy in the next few days. Choose one that is easy, one moderately difficult and two that are more difficult for you to do. For example, you might choose someone you had a disagreement with or who did something you didn't like. But this is the very person who needs you to reach out, who needs to be loved. And *you* will grow by taking the extra effort to reach out to this person.

Questions to ask yourself

1) Do you normally find yourself avoiding or going after opportunities to show love to someone with whom there have been difficulties?

2) Are there certain types of people you have trouble reaching out to?

3) Why is it easier for you to reach out to others?

4) What can you do to practice reaching out to the *difficult* people in your life?

Bringing happiness

Name of person	What can you do to bring happiness?	Is this easy or difficult?	What was the result?
1)			
2)			
3)			
4)			

5)   What happened when you did reach out to the difficult person?

Ground-breaking research by Elizabeth V. Dunn[28] gives more insights into how giving to others brings happiness. People reported greater happiness when they spent money on others or gave to charities than when they spent money on themselves. In another study,[29] she found higher levels of happiness when someone interacted with a stranger versus a romantic partner. The reason? More energy was put into the encounter with the stranger. Therefore Dunn concluded we feel best when we are pleasant and charming. So the old adage, *It is better to give than to receive,* turns out to be true on many levels, as discussed in chapter 1.

Love energizes and uplifts

For a man who has love, effort is a rest. He will travel any distance to visit his friends.[30]

Joy gives us wings! In times of joy our strength is more vital, our intellect keener, and our understanding less clouded. We seem better able to cope with the world and to find our sphere of usefulness. But when sadness visits us we become weak, our strength leaves us, our comprehension is dim and our intelligence veiled . . . and we become even as dead beings.
There is no human being untouched by these two influences; but all the sorrow and the grief that exist come from the world of matter – the spiritual world bestows only the joy![31]

Love is light in whatsoever house it may shine and enmity is darkness in whatsoever abode it dwell.[32]

When love is realized and the ideal spiritual bonds unite the hearts of men, the whole human race will be uplifted, the world will continually grow more spiritual and radiant and the happiness and tranquillity of mankind be immeasurably increased.[33]

Exercise

1) What do you feel when you are happy? Be specific about a range of emo-
    tions. What are you thinking about yourself, life, others? How do you
    behave?

2) What happens when you are down, unhappy? What do you think about
    yourself and others?

3) What are some ways to help you feel uplifted when you are down?

4) Think back to some times that you felt down. What were the things that led
    to your sad or despondent feelings?

5) What things can you do to bring happiness and joy to yourself?

6) Using the box on page 23, make a schedule for the next week of one thing
    you can do every day to gain happiness. At the end of the week, assess how
    you did and how your actions affected you.

Gaining happiness

Day of week	What can you do to bring yourself joy?	When did you accomplish the task?	What was the result of your task?
Sunday			
Monday			
Tuesday			
Wednesday			
Thursday			
Friday			
Saturday			

Exercise

1) Rank order the people below in terms of how happy you think someone from that group would generally be. Give a '1' to the most happy and '4' to the least happy.

     a)   Lottery winners (one year after winning) _____

     b)   Inuit from Greenland _____

     c)   Amish from Pennsylvania _____

     d)   College students _____

2) Check your answers in the endnote at the back of this book.[34]

3) List some reasons why you think these groups are ordered in this way.

According to research,[35] the Amish are most happy because their expectations for happiness are lower, they have a tight community and their strong belief in God (people who believe in God generally report higher levels of happiness) causes them to be grateful. The Inuit have similar reasons and, in addition, the harsh conditions make them more grateful for what they do have. College students are in a hopeful time in their lives, with many opportunities ahead, but they don't have the solid community of the Amish or Inuit. Lottery winners thought winning all that money would solve their problems but a year later they'd often spent all or much of it, sometimes they had huge debts, and their interpersonal dynamics had been poor because so many people had come to them for money.

Story: Living and loving to the fullest

I grew up in New York City, next door to Sharon, from first grade through high school. Most people never even knew she had cystic fibrosis because she would never complain about it or talk about it. She never wanted to make anyone feel bad for her. She just wanted to enjoy her life as best she could, even though she always knew her life would be short. If I had to choose one quality she embodied, it would be love. Love of others, herself and life in general. And I am convinced that the level of love she exhibited gave her supreme happiness.

We had camp outs in a pup tent in our backyard, we had a pulley between the decks and we would leave notes for each other. We played duets – Sharon on her clarinet and me on the saxophone. We were in Brownies and took baton lessons together. It was a childhood full of memories.

She played three varsity sports in high school (tennis, basketball and softball). She was an avid New York Mets fan and sent herself to Mets Fantasy Camp. It was definitely a fulfilled dream for her. She loved Lou Gramm, the lead singer of the rock group Foreigner. She also loved to play blackjack and eat Chinese food and shrimp.

Leaving the familiar East Coast when I graduated from high school, I ventured to Vanderbilt University for my undergraduate studies. I had never been that far from home before and I remember making the drive home one vacation and thinking about the song 'Take me Home, Country Roads'. Nashville, Tennessee, was very much 'country' to me.

During my four years at Vanderbilt Sharon visited me from New York. We went to 'music row' and did karaoke to 'Take Me Home, Country Roads'. She was the lead singer and I sang backup. We both have horrible singing voices and really destroyed the song!

Last year Sharon died in her fight with cystic fibrosis.

I have two children of my own and whenever they ask me to tell them a story about when I was a little girl, the story always includes Sharon. Sharon never married because she never wanted to ask someone else to 'put up' with her illness. She definitely lived her life to the fullest. She took vacations whenever she could, and did adventurous things like parasailing. Sharon told me to celebrate her life when she was gone. I miss her. I treasure the karaoke tape we made of 'Take Me Home, Country Roads' and think of her especially when I hear that song.

Jan Brottman, Full-time mother
Palatine, Illinois

3 Trustworthiness, Wisdom and Speaking Kindly of Others

I do not want the peace that
passeth understanding. I want the
understanding which bringeth peace.
Helen Keller

Love on its own, without other virtues, can be hollow. How difficult it is to love someone who is untrustworthy. I remember a client once complaining to me, 'Tell the employees to cut us some slack. They have to start trusting us.' My response, 'They'll begin to trust you as soon as you act in a trustworthy manner.' It's not reasonable to expect others to act better than you do yourself. As for our own behavior, we all have strengths and weaknesses. Martin Seligman's research shows it is better for your mental health and well-being to focus on your strengths, your core values and virtues, rather than obsessing about your flaws and weaknesses. In his book *Authentic Happiness*, he identifies 24 main strengths/virtues in six categories:

1) Wisdom (curiosity, love of learning, judgment, ingenuity, social intelligence, perspective)[1]

2) Courage (valor, perseverance, integrity)

3) Love and humanity (kindness, generosity, nurturance, and the capacity to love and be loved)

4) Temperance (modesty, humility, self-control, prudence, caution)

5) Justice (good citizenship, fairness, loyalty, teamwork, humane leadership)

6)   Transcendence (appreciation of beauty, gratitude, hope, spirituality, for-giveness, humor, zest)

The importance of virtues

Happy is the man that findeth wisdom, and the man that getteth understanding.[2]

. . . the foundation principles of the teachings of His Holiness Christ were mercy, love, fellowship, benevolence, altruism, the resplendence or radiance of divine bestowals, acquisition of the breaths of the Holy Spirit and oneness with God.[3]

One is the fundamental basis which comprises all spiritual things . . . it is spiritual and not material truth; it is faith, knowledge, certitude, justice, piety, righteousness, trustworthiness, love of God, benevo-lence, purity, detachment, humility, meekness, patience and con-stancy. It shows mercy to the poor, defends the oppressed, gives to the wretched and uplifts the fallen.[4]

Say: Honesty, virtue, wisdom and a saintly character redound to the exaltation of man, while dishonesty, imposture, ignorance and hypocrisy lead to his abasement. By My life! Man's distinction lieth not in ornaments or wealth, but rather in virtuous behavior and true understanding.[5]

Exercise

Part 1

Go to www.authentichappiness.sas.upenn.edu, which is the web site for Martin Seligman's work on positive psychology. Take the 'Brief Strengths Test' online and learn what your scores are. You may also choose to also take these instru-ments: a) GRIT Survey (measures character strength of perseverance), and b) VIA Signature Strengths.

Questions

1) What are your strengths?

2) Do you see any patterns on scores from several instruments?

3) What surprised you in the results?

4) Which results did you more or less expect?

Part 2

Complete the table on page 29. Fill in the boxes, as indicated. Choose among your peak strengths and the ones you enjoy using the most.

Questions

1) What was it like to use your strengths? How did it make you feel? What were the results?

2) How can you find the places of greatest potential that will utilize your strengths?

3) What are the things you spend your energies on, where instead of your strengths, you are playing from your weaknesses? What is the result?

4) How can you make sure you choose situations where your strengths are needed and can be of service?

Strengths

Name of strength	How you've used it in the past	What situations can you place yourself in where your strength will be fully utilized?
1)		
2)		
3)		
4)		
5)		

Love can bring other virtues and happiness

Love is the source of all the bestowals of God. Until love takes possession of the heart no other divine bounty can be revealed in it.[6]

Make their hearts good and pure in order that they may become
worthy of Thy love.[7]

The hearts should be purified and cleansed from every trace of
hatred and rancor and enabled to engage in truthfulness, conciliation,
uprightness and love toward the world of humanity . . .[8]

Let nothing grieve thee, and be thou angered at none. It behooveth
thee to be content with the Will of God, and a true and loving and
trusted friend to all the peoples of the earth, without any exceptions
whatever. This is the quality of the sincere, the way of the saints . . .[9]

Whoever has virtue and insight,
who is just, truthful, and does one's own work,
the world will love.[10]

Lack of love and virtues brings darkness

. . . if we meet with lying, faithlessness, and deceit, we are miserable.[11]

Know, verily, the heart wherein the least remnant of envy yet lingers,
shall never attain My everlasting dominion . . .[12]

Virtues bring loftiness

The virtuous are happy in this world,
and they are happy in the next; they are happy in both.
They are happy when they think of the good they have done.
They are even happier when going on the good path.[13]

. . . happiness is the attainment of spiritual perfections.[14]

They have not properly understood that man's supreme honor and real happiness lie in self-respect, in high resolves and noble purposes, in integrity and moral quality, in immaculacy of mind. They have, rather, imagined that their greatness consists in the accumulation, by whatever means may offer, of worldly goods.[15]

Qualities such as unselfishness, pity, kindness, fidelity, forbearance, forgiveness develop a sense of solidarity and establish concord. Under their influence men become ever more ready to relieve, to help and to uplift one another and labor with increasing earnestness to build a social order in which even justice shall be done, wrongs shall be redressed and the spirit of fraternity shall become the rule of life. Compassion and goodwill create an environment which itself aids their own further growth.[16]

Overcome anger by love; overcome wrong by good;
overcome the miserly by generosity, and the liar by truth.[17]

Exercise

Think of two times when you've been extremely happy and two times when you've been extremely unhappy. List down the circumstances for each, as shown in the table on page 32.

Questions to ask yourself

1) What makes you more likely to use your strengths than weaknesses? Are there certain conditions present?

2) When are you more likely to use your weaknesses? How can you learn to use strengths instead?

3) How can you put yourself in more situations that require your strengths?

Happiness and unhappiness

Situation happy: Describe	Were you using strengths or weaknesses? Which ones?	What made you so happy?	How could you have used even more of your strengths?
1)			
2)			

Situation unhappy: Describe	Were you using strengths or weaknesses? Which ones?	What made you so unhappy?	How could you have used strengths instead of weaknesses?
3)			
4)			

Justice and love are both important

Justice, love and kindness must be the instruments of strength, not of weakness.[18]

The best beloved of all things in My sight is Justice . . . By its aid thou shalt see with thine own eyes and not through the eyes of others, and shalt know of thine own knowledge and not through the knowledge of thy neighbor.[19]

How to recognize virtues

For every thing, however, God has created a sign and symbol, and established standards and tests by which it may be known. The spiritually learned must be characterized by both inward and outward perfections; they must possess a good character, an enlightened nature, a pure intent, as well as intellectual power, brilliance and discernment, intuition, discretion and foresight, temperance, reverence, and a heartfelt fear of God. For an unlit candle, however great in diameter and tall, is no better than a barren palm tree or a pile of dead wood.[20]

Trustworthiness, wisdom and honesty are, of a truth, God's beauteous adornments for His creatures. These fair garments are a befitting vesture for every temple. Happy are those that comprehend, and well is it with them that acquire such virtue.[21]

Backbiting is hurtful

Better keep yourself clean and bright; you are the window through which you must see the world. *George Bernard Shaw*

It's much easier to see how harmful backbiting is when you are the target. It hurts and the pain stays for a long, long time. For myself, I've noticed that my desire to backbite is set off when I have a conflict with someone or a person does something that bothers me. But if I have the courage to talk to that person directly, my 'need' to backbite disappears. Of course, a higher level of development would be that I never even think about backbiting, and that's what I'm working towards.

> For he that will love life, and see good days, let him refrain his tongue from evil, and his lips that they speak no guile: Let him eschew evil, and do good; let him seek peace, and ensue it.[22]

> Each of us is responsible for one life only, and that is our own. Each of us is immeasurably far from being 'perfect as our heavenly father is perfect' and the task of perfecting our own life and character is one that requires all our attention, our will-power and energy . . . abstain from fault-finding, while being ever eager to discover and root out our own faults and overcome our own failings.[23]

> The worst human quality and the most great sin is backbiting . . .[24]

> . . . the most hateful characteristic of man is fault-finding. One must expose the praiseworthy qualities of the souls and not their evil attributes. The friends must overlook their shortcomings and faults and speak only of their virtues and not their defects.[25]

> Breathe not the sins of others so long as thou art thyself a sinner. Shouldst thou transgress this command, accursed wouldst thou be, and to this I bear witness.[26]

> Never speak disparagingly of others, but praise without distinction. Pollute not your tongues by speaking evil of another.[27]

> If one speaks or acts with a pure thought,
> happiness follows one,
> like a shadow that never leaves.[28]

Strive towards wisdom and virtues

> My Lord! Vouchsafe me wisdom and unite me to the righteous.[29]

The one I call holy has deep wisdom and knowledge,
discerns the right way and the wrong,
and has attained the highest end.[30]

We beg of God to assist the children of His loved ones and adorn
them with wisdom, good conduct, integrity and righteousness.[31]

Therefore you must thank God that He has bestowed upon you the
blessing of life and existence in the human kingdom. Strive diligently
to acquire virtues befitting [you] . . . When man is not endowed with
inner perception he is not informed of these important mysteries. The
retina of outer vision though sensitive and delicate may nevertheless
be a hindrance to the inner eye which alone can perceive.[32]

Pray to God that He may strengthen you in divine virtue, so that you
may be as angels in the world, and beacons of light to disclose the
mysteries of the Kingdom to those with understanding hearts.[33]

The fool who knows one's own folly,
is wise at least to that extent;
but the fool who thinks oneself wise is really a fool.[34]

Exercise

Think about the situations you described above, in the previous two exercises,
which had you look at when you use your strengths.

Questions to ask yourself

1) What happens when you use your strengths compared to when you operate
   from your weaknesses?

2) How can you learn to employ your strengths more often?

3) What did you learn about yourself from these exercises?

Story: Wisdom gained

I thought I was pretty savvy with money. During the 90s I studied the stock market, particularly the companies in Seattle, where I was then based, and I made a lot of money. It felt good to be financially secure.

Then I moved to North Carolina into an extremely demanding job and was unable to give the same attention to my portfolio. Adding to my worry was the fact that the stock market was starting a downturn and I didn't know how to handle that.

As luck would have it, a close friend called, raving on about her financial advisor and how much money he had made for her in recent years. My friend had been a single mother for many years. She was a physician and, like me, had no one else to manage her money.

When I talked to the advisor, he sounded so competent and he kept saying that he understood how difficult it was for a single woman like me to shoulder all of this financial burden myself. He knew my vulnerabilities and my friend's. I put about 70 per cent of my money with this guy.

He immediately sold all my stocks and put them in emerging high-risk companies, which shortly tanked. But that paper loss wasn't the worst part. I soon got a bill from IRS for $100,000 for capital gains taxes. How did I not know about this? And why didn't the financial advisor talk me through this mine field? I knew I had been duped and quickly got what was left of my portfolio out of his hands.

Now, most people would have learned from this, would have become wise. But not me. A few years later I moved to Albuquerque, still limping financially from those losses. So when a colleague at work sent around an email about how he had been collecting choice mountain properties and was offering them to a select few, taking $50,000 off the appraised price of $220,000, I took the bait. Though the land was difficult to get to, my colleague assured me the prices would be going up on this steal-of-a-deal land. When I balked at the location, he called me at 6 a.m. to tell me how much money I was going to make.

One week before closing, I got a strong sense something was wrong and called three real estate agents, who all said the land was way overpriced and I should kill the deal. So I called my colleague the day before closing to say that I was pulling out.

He started to cry. 'You made a commitment,' he scolded me. 'This is like a marriage, you have to hang in there.' He went on about how the money was for his mother's nursing home bills and how her Alzheimer's would get worse if he had to move her out. 'You are getting cold feet. This is just buyer's remorse.'

I kept my resolve and told him the deal was not worth it. So he came back with stronger weapons.

'I am more connected at work than you are, the new person, and I can make your life difficult when I tell people how untrustworthy you've been.' He offered to take $10,000 off the purchase price.

Now when I look back, I can't believe I went through with the deal. If I had thought about it, I would have realized that, in fact, I had better relationships at work than he did, as he was only a part-timer. So now I have some mountain property that I won't be able to sell for at least 10 years.

What have I learned from this? To be wiser in my financial dealings, to ask around more, both about the person and about the deal, and to beware, be wary, of anyone who tries to pull my heart strings, who manipulates me by going after my weaknesses. Maybe all of this happened so that I would gain more wisdom. I'm sure wiser now. Nothing similar has happened for years, so I think I have learned my lesson.

Laura Parker, VP for Product Development
Albuquerque, New Mexico

4 Love and Forgiveness

To forgive oneself? No, that doesn't work:
we have to be forgiven. But we can only believe
this is possible if we ourselves can forgive.
Dag Hammarskjöld

The insistent self is really good at coaching itself to nurse past hurts, to hold grudges and to seek revenge. Not only does such behavior wreak havoc on relationships but it is also bad for your health. Several major studies have shown that people who forgive others have more peace of mind, less illness and live longer.[1] What keeps people from forgiving? It might be the insistent self, which demands a certain type of conduct from others, an unwillingness to let go and move on, a deep need to feel angry at others or, as a recent study found, an expectation of special treatment and a preoccupation with defending one's rights. How ironic that the behavior of not forgiving, which relates to a type of self-defense, actually makes you worse off and therefore undefended.

Forgiveness is divine

Let all bitterness, and wrath, and anger, and clamor, and evil speaking, be put away from you, with all malice. And be ye kind one to another, tenderhearted, forgiving one another, even as God for Christ's sake hath forgiven you.[2]

For Christ declared: 'Love your enemies, and pray for them that persecute you that you may be sons of your Father which is in Heaven; for He maketh His sun to rise on the evil and the good, and sendeth rain on the just and the unjust.' How can hatred, hostility and persecution be reconciled with Christ and His teachings?[3]

Forgive and overlook the shortcomings which have appeared in that one, for the sake of love and affection.[4]

Forgive, be of service and love

> But true love does not ignore all faults and failings: on the contrary, it
> scans them keenly, though only in order to be able to understand, to
> explain, and thus to excuse them.[5]

> I now try to serve those in need without expecting recognition, to
> forgive those who may have offended me without holding grudges and
> to share with others what I have learned, and thereby contribute to
> my own happiness and theirs.[6]

> No, rather he must return good for evil, and not only forgive, but also,
> if possible, be of service to his oppressor. This conduct is worthy of
> man: for what advantage does he gain by vengeance? The two actions
> are equivalent; if one action is reprehensible, both are reprehensible.
> The only difference is that one was committed first, the other later.[7]

> There is only one great verity in it: Love, the mainspring of every
> energy, tolerance toward each other, desire of understanding each
> other, knowing each other, helping each other, forgiving each other.[8]

Exercise

Go to www.authentichappiness.sas.upenn.edu and take the Transgression Motivation Questionnaire, which measures forgiveness.

Questions to ask yourself

1) Were you average, above average or below average?

2) Did your scores surprise you?

3) What steps can you take to get better scores?

4) Would it have mattered if you had thought of someone else when you took the questionnaire? How?

Instantly forgive

If some one commits an error and wrong toward you, you must instantly forgive him. Do not complain of others. Refrain from reprimanding them, and if you wish to give admonition or advice, let it be offered in such a way that it will not burden the bearer. Turn all your thoughts toward bringing joy to hearts. Beware! Beware! lest ye offend any heart.[9]

We must look upon our enemies with a sin-covering eye and act with justice when confronted with any injustice whatsoever, forgive all, consider the whole of humanity as our own family, the whole earth as our own country, be sympathetic with all suffering, nurse the sick, offer a shelter to the exiled, help the poor and those in need, dress all wounds and share the happiness of each one. Be compassionate, so that your actions will shine like unto the light [10]

. . . of the civilizing of human behavior: . . .'who master their anger, and forgive others!'[11]

But if he who has been struck pardons and forgives, he shows the greatest mercy. This is worthy of admiration.[12]

Forgive and forget

Forgive thy neighbor the hurt that he hath done unto thee,
so shall thy sins also be forgiven when thou prayest.[13]

. . . to forgive and forget the past, and face the future with radiance and confidence.[14]

How can . . . Love be demonstrated . . . save by its capacity to endure to the uttermost the blows of calamity and darts of affliction, the hatred of enemies and the treachery of seeming friends, to rise serene above all these and, undismayed and unembittered, still to forgive and bless?[15]

Show ye an endeavor that all the nations and communities of the world, even the enemies, put their trust, assurance and hope in you; that if a person falls into errors for a hundred-thousand times he may yet turn his face to you, hopeful that you will forgive his sins; for he must not become hopeless, neither grieved nor despondent.[16]

You must follow the example and footprints of Jesus Christ. Read the Gospels. Jesus Christ was mercy itself, was love itself. He even prayed in behalf of His executioners − for those who crucified Him − saying, 'Father, forgive them; for they know not what they do.'[17]

Lowly, suppliant and fallen upon my face, I beseech Thee with all the ardor of my invocation to pardon whosoever hath hurt me, forgive him that hath conspired against me and offended me, and wash away the misdeeds of them that have wrought injustice upon me.[18]

Forgive us our sins.[19]

Forgive and overlook the shortcomings which have appeared in that one, for the sake of love and affection.[20]

Society − not the individual − punishes

If a person commit a crime against you, you have not the right to forgive him; but the law must punish him in order to prevent a repetition of that same crime by others, as the pain of the individual is unimportant beside the general welfare of the people.[21]

Beware of tyrants and thieves

> Then strive ye with heart and soul to practice love and kindness to
> the world of humanity at large, except to those souls who are selfish
> and insincere. It is not advisable to show kindness to a person who
> is a tyrant, a traitor or a thief because kindness encourages him to
> become worse and does not awaken him. The more kindness you
> show to a liar the more he is apt to lie, for he thinks that you know
> not, while you do know, but extreme kindness keeps you from reveal-
> ing your knowledge.[22]

Exercise

List in the table on page 43 people you feel have wronged you. Some of them
should be people you have forgiven and some for whom you still harbor a hurt
or anger. Then fill in the table.

1) Do you see any patterns in terms of which people you forgave and which
   you did not? Describe.

2) What advantage does it give you *not* to forgive (for example, you can feel
   self-righteous if you hold onto a grudge, you might feel superior because
   the person did something 'bad')?

3) What can you do to allow yourself to forgive?

4) How could forgiving make your life better?

Story: The gift of forgiveness

My parents had a disastrously unhappy marriage for most of the 20 years they
were together. In fact, they couldn't even live together for the last 13 years.

Forgiveness

Name	What they did	Forgave yes/no?	Why you did or did not forgive

Finally, they got the courage to divorce. I think part of their hesitation was about us kids, trying to 'stay together' for us, even though they weren't actually together most of the time.

After they divorced, each of them married younger partners, and though my parents were civil to one another (because of us, I am sure), we could all feel the tension between them. Within five years my father was diagnosed with cancer. Because my mother was a nurse, my father and his new wife moved in with my mother and her new husband. It was certainly a modern family! The miracle that occurred, though, was how my parents were able to get past their anger, their hurt. It was like they were reborn. They loved one another in a totally new way. Neither one expected the other to fill his or her emotional needs. My mother was there to serve, and my father was so grateful, he spent a lot of energy just making sure my mother was happy. And his new wife? She worshiped the ground my mother walked on. All four of them were such role models to us kids, the ones for whom they had covered up the truth during many years.

My father died a while back but his widow and my mother are now best friends. I contrast this to my Aunt Jane and Uncle Marty, who divorced before my parents did but never, ever spoke to each other afterwards. My cousin Barbara told me last year that she finally spent Christmas with her father, for the first time in 25 years, but she had to lie to her mother about it. Barbara was in tears, so torn between the two people she loved the most. And I wonder: if death can help bring people together and forgive, why can't we learn to do it without such an tremendous loss? With Marty and Jane, I doubt even this finality would have melted the pile upon pile of collected offenses. It is almost as if they had their resentments stored in accounts that were jealously guarded, to make sure the balance kept increasing. But with people like my parents, why wait until the end? If the capacity to forgive is there, why can't we use it before tragedy strikes?

Jonathan Norton
Wayzata, Minnesota

5 Appreciating vs. Judging

When someone receives us with open-hearted, non-judging, intensely interested listening, our spirits expand.
Sue Patton Thoele

It's actually quite easy to find fault with other people, to feel superior to them because of their beliefs, social class, ethnicity. However, such feelings do not lead to a sense of well-being. Jonathan Haidt's research on happiness[1] looked at where we can find the most bliss, and it isn't in creating an 'us vs. them' scenario. In one study he looked at liberals and conservatives, finding that liberals are very concerned about victimization of others, equality, rights of individuals (especially minorities and non-conformists), while conservatives are highly concerned with loyalty to the group, respect for authority and sacredness. While each side often demonizes the other, in actuality both sides are moral but in different ways. Balance is the key, he says. A society with only conservatives would tend to be callous and oppressive to some groups, while a society of strictly liberals would lose social structures and constrictions that are vital to a sustainable civilization. If either left or right dominates, the result is an imbalance in our communities. Haidt tells us that real and long-lasting happiness comes from the balance of old and new, east and west, conservative and liberal. Rather than castigating the other side, our best hope is in seeing good in opponents, in learning rather than judging.[2]

Love requires an open heart, not being judgmental

Love Me, that I may love thee. If thou lovest Me not, My love can in no wise reach thee.[3]

Love the creatures for the sake of God and not for themselves. You will never become angry or impatient if you love them for the sake of God . . . There are imperfections in every human being, and you will always become unhappy if you look toward the people themselves . . .

Therefore, do not look at the shortcomings of anybody; see with the sight of forgiveness.[4]

Treat others with kindness

Be not forgetful to entertain strangers: for thereby some have entertained angels unawares.[5]

A greater degree of love will produce a greater unity, because it enables people to bear with each other, to be patient and forgiving.[6]

Necessarily there will be some who are defective amongst men, but it is our duty to enable them by kind methods of guidance and teaching to become perfected . . . But all this must be accomplished in the spirit of kindness and love and not by strife, antagonism nor in a spirit of hostility and hatred, for this is contrary to the good pleasure of God. That which is acceptable in the sight of God is love.[7]

Be kindly affectioned one to another with brotherly love; in honor preferring one another.[8]

Cooperation is preferable to competition

Let us cooperate in love and through spiritual reciprocity enjoy eternal happiness and peace.[9]

Appreciative inquiry

David Cooperrider[10] has found that positive change comes more quickly when people ask questions to try to find out what works, what is good, rather than focusing on diagnosing the negative part of problems. Similarly, Chris Argyris[11] talks about two kinds of interpersonal communication: advocacy (when you are explaining or arguing your position) and inquiry (when you ask sincere, open-ended questions). To really understand another person and reduce defenses, it is better to ask lots of questions. Bahiyyih Nakhjavani in her book *Asking Questions*[12] says we need to redefine our notion of questions. Instead of providing conclusive responses, questions can become an aid in creating more open minds, bringing humility in answers, which move towards solutions that might even be paradoxical.

Exercise

Outcome-Directed Thinking (from Bostrom & Associates)[13]

1)   Think of a problem you have in your life (work, friends or family), a problem to which you have difficulty finding a solution. Write it below.

2)   Answer the following questions regarding this problem.

    a)   Who caused it?

    b)   When did it start?

    c)   What conditions existed that made this situation happen?

    d)   Is there someone you should hold accountable?

    e)   Assess how you feel after answering the above questions? Do you feel uplifted and ready to solve the problem or rather down about the whole thing?

3)   Consider the same problem. Now answer the questions below.

    a)   What would you rather have instead of this situation? What would be your ideal outcome?

b) What steps can you take to achieve your desired outcome? List
    them in the chart on page 49 and when you can do them.

c) How was this different from answering the questions in no. 2
    above? Were you more or less enthused about solving the prob-
    lem?

d) Which of the techniques (problem analysis or outcome-directed)
    do you think is most helpful in solving a problem?

According to Bostrom & Associates, most people report that the outcome-
directed thinking is more energizing and helps them come to a better solution.
Using the first method, they feel dragged down by the problem itself.

   This exercise can be used individually or with groups. It helps people see
how important focusing on the positive outcomes is for harnessing energy and
enthusiasm to solve problems.

Love requires appreciation, inquiry and seeing others as equals

Therefore we must emulate and follow the divine policy, dealing with
each other in the utmost love and tenderness.[14]

Read, in the school of God, the lessons of the spirit, and learn from
love's Teacher the innermost truths.[15]

This heavenly food is knowledge, understanding, faith, assurance,
love, affinity, kindness, purity of purpose, attraction of hearts and the
union of souls.[16]

God has endowed us with intellects, not for the purpose of making
instruments of destruction; but that we might become diffusers of
light; create love between the hearts; establish communion between
the spirits and bring together the people of the east and the west.[17]

Your desired outcome:

Actions needed to achieve outcome that you will do	When you will do them	List help you'll need and from whom
1)		
2)		
3)		
4)		

We must be united. We must love each other. We must ever praise each other. We must bestow commendation upon all people, thus removing the discord and hatred which have caused alienation amongst men. Otherwise, the conditions of the past will continue, praising ourselves and condemning others; religious wars will have no end and religious prejudice, the prime cause of this havoc and tribulation, will increase.[18]

You must manifest complete love and affection toward all mankind. Do not exalt yourselves above others, but consider all as your equals, recognizing them as the servants of one God. Know that God is compassionate toward all; therefore, love all from the depths of your hearts, prefer all religionists to yourselves, be filled with love for every race, and be kind toward the people of all nationalities.[19]

Questions bring clarity and understanding

Verily, as you reflect deeply, ponder deliberately and think continually, the doors of knowledge will be opened unto you.[20]

Ponder this in thine heart, that the truth may be revealed unto thee . . .[21]

Ponder a while thereon, that with both your inner and outer eye, ye may perceive the subtleties of Divine wisdom and discover the gems of heavenly knowledge . . .[22]

Ponder and reflect.[23]

Exercise

Part I: Situation past

1) Think of a conflict you recently had with someone. Jot down some notes about it below, noting what was said on both sides.

2) Rewrite the script. Think of questions you could have asked the person to help you understand the issues better and therefore come to a more acceptable solution.

HELPFUL QUESTIONS

    a) Tell me your reasoning behind this.

    b) Help me to see the holes in my argument.

    c) Give me some ways I can understand your position more clearly.

    d) Can you summarize for me the main points?

    e) How can I understand your position better?

    f) What am I missing from the points you are making?

    g) Do you see any blocks or defenses in the way I am thinking?

    h) What questions would you like me to ask you, so that I can understand you better?

UNHELPFUL QUESTIONS

    a) Can't you see where you are wrong?

b) Why you can't see it my way?

c) Don't you think that . . . ? (this is a thinly veiled attempt to get your point across, not to find out the other's opinion)

d) Why are you being so unreasonable?

QUESTIONS TO ASK YOURSELF

a) How would you expect the interaction to change if you started asking such questions?

b) Why do you think people use advocacy (stating your own position) rather than ask questions?

c) What's the advantage of advocacy? Of questions?

3) How can you learn to ask more questions?

Part II: Situation future

Think of a conflict you are having with someone that hasn't been resolved. Based on the information above, what kinds of questions could you ask the other person?

1) Write your questions below:

a)

b)

c)

d)

e)

2) Ask a trusted friend to read over your questions, to make sure they are in the spirit of true inquiry. Do a role-play with your friend, to practice answering the questions.

3) Get together with the person with whom you are having the problem. Go with the attitude of searching for the truth, in order to solve the problem. Don't go with the idea that you already know the solution and have to convince the other person to correct their conclusions. Try to be ready to ask, listen and search for the truth with an open mind.

QUESTIONS TO ASK YOURSELF

a) How often do you try and resolve problems with a closed mind? What do you tell yourself about why your position is the correct one?

b) How can you get yourself to practice asking more questions? What are some reminders you can use for yourself?

c) What difference is there when you ask open-ended questions compared with asking questions to which you want a certain answer?

d) Do you remember having a teacher who asked questions but expected only one answer? What was it like to be on the receiving end?

Story: The boy who needed love

I am the director of an after-school program at a public school in Brooklyn, as well as a drama instructor at the weekend Children's Theater Company (CTC). This is a four-part program in drama, dance, music and ethical education in which children perform in productions that focus on global issues.

In the public school program I met an adorable student, nine year old Martin, whom I got to know very well and very quickly because he was constantly 'in trouble', spending more time in the principal's office than in class. Martin is not a 'bad kid'; he just has severe ADHD and has problems listening and following directions – but smart as a whip! One day he actually said to me, 'I'm having difficulty controlling my motor skills. I need to tell my brain to communicate better with my arms and legs.'

Martin lives with his devoted father but his mother is a mess. Even though she lives four blocks away, she rarely sees him, and when she does, her parenting skills are poor, at best. She has repeatedly changed her phone number without telling him, leaving him with a feeling of abandonment every time he tries to call only to hear, 'The number you are trying to reach has been disconnected'.

Martin copes with his pain through displays of misbehavior. One day he told me (and, yes, these were his exact words), 'I'm seeking attention and since I can't get it through positive means, I seek it through negativity.'

The kids in his school and in my after-school program did not like him and the teachers often saw him as yet another 'problem child'. The school principal and I reached out to him in many ways but the way that finally worked was the day I enrolled him in my Saturday program at the Children's Theatre Company.

Because the culture was so inclusive, Martin felt accepted by other kids for the first time in his life. The kids at CTC didn't seem to notice his uncontrollable body parts or hyper-activity and the teachers took him under their wing quickly; within several weeks, two of the CTC mothers approached the director and asked if they could 'adopt' Martin on Saturdays and be his CTC 'moms'. All I can say is he was loved and appreciated. Not present were the snide remarks he was used to, the name-calling, the eye-rolling or the negative feedback from teachers and parents.

Today, Martin's behavior is barely recognizable. We took the CTC kids to a retreat center and Martin voluntarily signed up for every service project task from cafeteria clean-up to vacuuming, and he performed each task with the utmost zeal, care and pride. Everyone fell in love with him. Two months ago the principal at the public school expressed her pride at seeing such a transformation in a student. Martin doesn't get 'in trouble' as much anymore, though he still bounces off the wall.

'CTC performed a miracle,' his father said.

No, I thought, we just loved Martin for who he is.

Jill Bostridge, Co-Artistic Director
of the Children's Theatre Company
New York City

6 Knowing and Loving Yourself

*Not until we are lost
do we begin to understand ourselves.*
Henry David Thoreau

I've heard people say it is selfish to love yourself. But just the opposite is true. Psychologists have shown us that whatever we feel towards ourselves gets projected out onto other people. So, if you don't like yourself, you are going to find a lot of people you don't like. If you are angry at yourself, you'll be angry to others. Parents often 'hand down' emotions from their parents. If they felt abandoned, they are more likely to emotionally abandon their own children. One way to break that cycle is to become aware of your inner emotions, your inner needs. Learning this can help you to become more loving, more giving and, ultimately, happier.

Knowledge of self brings freedom

And that by their freedom from enslavement, their knowledge, their self-control, they shall be first among the pure, the free and the wise.[1]

Self-consciousness accompanies individualized character, and the being thus endowed has the potentiality of rising to the knowledge of God.[2]

True loss is for him whose days have been spent in utter ignorance of his self.[3]

The soul of the ungoverned is not his,
Nor hath he knowledge of himself; which lacked,
How grows serenity? and, wanting that,
Whence shall he hope for happiness?[4]

Better to develop the higher self

Self has really two meanings, or is used in two senses . . . one is self, the identity of the individual created by God. This is the self mentioned in such passages as 'he hath known God who hath known himself', etc. The other self is the ego, the dark, animalistic heritage each one of us has, the lower nature that can develop into a monster of selfishness, brutality, lust and so on. It is this self we must struggle against, or this side of our natures, in order to strengthen and free the spirit within us and help it to attain perfection.[5]

Blessed art thou for having utterly abolished the idol of self and of vain imagination, and for having rent asunder the veil of idle fancy . . .[6]

Life is a constant struggle, not only against forces around us, but above all against our own 'ego'. We can never afford to rest on our oars, for if we do, we soon see ourselves carried down stream again.[7]

Man's pride in his accomplishments, his knowledge, his position, his popularity within society and, above all, his love for his own self are some of the barriers which come between him and God.[8]

Knowledge and learning create self esteem

Apart from the acquisition of knowledge and moral values conducive to social evolution, education provides such benefits as the development of the mind, and training in logical and analytical thinking, organizational, administrative and management skills, as well as enhanced self esteem and improved status within the community.[9]

We cannot bring love and unity to pass merely by talking of it. Knowledge is not enough. Wealth, science, education are good, we know: but we must also work and study to bring to maturity the fruit of knowledge.[10]

There is always movement and growth

> . . . man should know his own self and recognize that which leadeth
> unto loftiness or lowliness, glory or abasement, wealth or poverty.[11]

People want to grow, to advance, as any parent knows who's had a teenager
reach driving age. Even at work, people want to grow. One study showed the
top reason given for quitting professional jobs was: 'I wasn't learning enough.'
It's the same with friendships. They begin to feel stale if there is no growth.
I changed careers a few years ago, and even though I was completely over-
whelmed trying to keep up, I found the learning exhilarating.

> Praise be to God! man is always turned toward the heights, and his
> aspiration is lofty; he always desires to reach a greater world than
> the world in which he is, and to mount to a higher sphere than that
> in which he is. The love of exaltation is one of the characteristics of
> man.[12]

> . . . every man will advance and develop until he attaineth the station
> at which he can manifest all the potential forces with which his inmost
> true self hath been endowed.[13]

The importance of wisdom

Studies[14] show that people with higher levels of wisdom are less likely to
engage in pleasure-seeking behaviors or thirst for the ultimate comfortable
life, instead preferring activities that revolve around personal growth, environmental protection and societal engagement. They showed greater levels of
empathy. High wisdom people also did not like conflict resolution strategies
where one side 'won' or dominated, but rather tended towards collaborative
approaches.

> All over the world one hears beautiful sayings extolled and noble pre-
> cepts admired. All men say they love what is good, and hate every-
> thing that is evil! Sincerity is to be admired, whilst lying is despicable.
> Faith is a virtue, and treachery is a disgrace to humanity. It is a blessed
> thing to gladden the hearts of men, and wrong to be the cause of

pain. To be kind and merciful is right, while to hate is sinful. Justice is a noble quality and injustice an iniquity. That it is one's duty to be pitiful and harm no one, and to avoid jealousy and malice at all costs. Wisdom is the glory of man, not ignorance; light, not darkness![15]

Exercise

Refer back to your results from the Strengths tests taken in chapter 3 on virtues (or go to www.authentichappiness.sas.upenn.edu to take the test). In this case look only at your wisdom scores, which include curiosity, love of learning, judgment, ingenuity, social intelligence, perspective. Choose your two strongest wisdom characteristics. Think of several situations when you have acted with and without wisdom, specifically with and without those two characteristics of wisdom. Fill out the table on page 60.

Story: Just the way you are

Each year, my father, a physician, would take one of his children with him to a medical convention as a special trip. I went to Miami with my father and uncle (also a physician) when I was 15 in 1978. While they attended seminars during the day, I would lounge by the pool. My siblings had inherited my father's dark Colombian looks but I was a carbon copy of my fair-skinned east Tennessee mother. In fact, another doctor in our community who was very good friends with my father never believed I was my father's child. He was Cuban and would say whenever he visited, 'Now, which neighbor do you belong to? I know you are not one of Luis's children!' I tried quick tanning solutions but they just turned me streaky orange. I thought Miami would be my chance. I tried so hard to get a tan and have the beautiful copper glaze that came so naturally to my six brothers and sisters but I just got very sunburned from the day I spent in the sun.

To cheer me up, my father and uncle took me to the hotel lounge that night to dance. They kept bragging to the other doctors about what a beautiful daughter/niece they had, even when my face was as red as a lobster. When they played Billy Joel's '[I Love You] Just the Way You Are' my father asked me to dance and tried to sing the refrain to me. He told me I didn't need to look like anyone but myself; he loved me just the way I was. I believed him because I looked like my mother. And he loved her enough to marry her. I never tried

Strengths

Situations	What were the results?	Other strengths you could have used here
in which I used _____ strength:		
in which I used _____ the other wisdom strength:		
in which I did not use _____ strength:		
in which I did not use _____ the other wisdom strength:		

to 'look Hispanic' again and I can never hear that song without thinking about dancing with my dad in Miami.

Nancy Ordoñez
Murfreesboro, Tennessee

7 Love, Hope and Transformation

*We look forward to the time when the
Power of Love will replace the Love of Power.
Then will our world know the blessings of peace.*
William E. Gladstone

Hope brings a better life

Some of the early writing on hope came from Austrian psychiatrist Viktor Frankl,[1] a World War II concentration camp survivor who noticed prisoners who survived did so because they had hope and a sense of purpose. They believed they could make a positive difference in someone's life and therefore they had the strength to endure the harsh and dehumanizing conditions. More recent research[2] shows that adults, adolescents and children who have higher levels of hope have enhanced lives, whether in relation to school or athletics, better health, superior problem-solving skills or being better adjusted psychologically. Other studies[3] show that when leaders, CEOs and leadership teams have higher levels of hopefulness, their organizations achieve greater employee job satisfaction. Also, scientists have shown[4] that hopefulness is a learnable skill and that through focused training people can raise their hope indices. Hope increases resilience, and both hope and resilience were shown to be instrumental in enabling people to make radical changes in their lives, such as leaving gang life, even when living in crime-infested neighborhoods. Finally, a recent study[5] showed that hope and social support were building blocks of life satisfaction.

Remain hopeful

Never lose thy trust in God! Be thou ever hopeful, for the bounties of God never cease to flow upon man. If viewed from one perspective they seem to decrease, but from another they are full and complete. Man is under all conditions immersed in a sea of God's blessings. Therefore, be thou not hopeless under any circumstances, but rather be firm in thy hope.[6]

Set all thy hope in God, and cleave tenaciously to His unfailing mercy.[7]

Create in me a pure heart, O my God, and renew a tranquil conscience within me, O my Hope![8]

O my Lord! Make Thy beauty to be my food, and Thy presence my drink, and Thy pleasure my hope, and praise of Thee my action, and remembrance of Thee my companion . . .[9]

Bring hope to others

Your greatest longing is to comfort those who mourn, to strengthen the weak, and to be the cause of hope to the despairing soul.[10]

Love brings hope to the hopeless and gladdens the hearts of the sorrowful.[11]

Exercise

Hope vs. hopelessness

1) Keep a journal, or put thoughts down in a notebook, of the statements you make each day that are either hopeful or hopeless. List each statement separately and write down the entire sentence. These statements include your thoughts as well as spoken comments.

2) After one week, fill out the table on page 64.

Questions to ask yourself

1) Did you have more hopeful or hopeless statements?

Hope

Statement	What preceded comment?	Hopeful or hopeless?	Said to myself or another?	What impact did the statement have?

2) Can you see any patterns in what happened right before you made hopeful
    statements? Before you made hopeless comments?

3) Were you more or less hopeful in comments to or about others?

4) What impact did your statements make?

5) What did you learn about yourself from this exercise?

The world is an illusion

For many years I have pondered the meaning of the phrase 'the world is an
illusion'. Did it mean my furniture is a figment of my imagination? That the
mountain I ski on could just as easily disappear in a flash of cosmic truth?
Recently I read an explanation that helped me understand this better. Jonathan
Haidt[12] talks about how the illusion of the world consists in the assumptions,
expectations, obligations, resentments, love or hate we have towards other
people. We put ourselves into a confined mental space where anger rages when
a loved one says the 'wrong' thing, when someone doesn't appreciate all the
work we have done, when a driver cuts in front, and so on and so on. If only we
could be content with whatever is ordained, go with the flow and understand
that much of our pain is caused by the way we look at things, the expectations
we put on others – only to be disappointed when they don't comply.

> If we suffer it is the outcome of material things, and all the trials and
> troubles come from this world of illusion.[13]

> O friend, the heart is the dwelling of eternal mysteries, make it not the
> home of fleeting fancies . . .[14]

> May the radiant sea of reality become clear and unveiled of its clouds;
> may people become freed from the quagmires of the world of matter

and soar upward to the city of light.[15]

The world is but a show, vain and empty, a mere nothing, bearing the
semblance of reality.[16]

Know ye that the world is like unto a mirage which the thirsty one
thinks to be water; its water is a vapor; its mercy a difficulty; its repose
hardship and ordeal; leave it to its people and turn unto the Kingdom
of your Lord the Merciful.[17]

Love can cause transformation

. . . religion must be the cause of fellowship and love. If it becomes
the cause of estrangement then it is not needed, for religion is like a
remedy; if it aggravates the disease then it becomes unnecessary.[18]

He also remarked that the way to broaden the outlook of the very
narrow-hearted and prejudiced . . . was by showing towards them the
greatest kindness and love.[19]

Story: Down on his luck

Last year I was standing for a few minutes outside the Borders bookstore in
New York City when I looked down and saw a man sitting on the sidewalk with
a book in his hands. Since New Yorkers often talk to one another, I struck up a
conversation and asked if he worked at the store. He looked at me and said, no,
he was homeless and was just reading near a warm building. Something about
him impressed me. He seemed articulate and educated, and so I wondered how
a guy like that ended up here.

My curiosity aroused, I asked if he wanted to go for a coffee. Reluctantly,
he agreed, but when we got there, it took lots of negotiating for him to let me
buy him some food, and then he'd only take a bagel. After a short time I could
see that this guy was normal but had had a run of bad luck. Nick's former girlfriend was wealthy and she convinced him to quit his night-shift job because
she worked days. 'Why pay rent?' she kept asking him, so he moved in with her.
Eighteen months later, when she decided to get back together with her doctor
boyfriend, Nick was out on the street with no job. His first night was spent in a

shelter but he was beaten up and had to have 56 stitches, so, understandably, he didn't go back there. Though he was clean and sober now, an affair with drugs during his short college career had set his family against him.

We talked all afternoon and I kept wondering how I could help him. He finally agreed to come to our house for dinner. When I called my husband, he just about hit the roof. Bringing a homeless guy to our house? But in the end, he agreed, as long as we were really careful. When Phil got home and met Nick, he too saw something special in him. It was below freezing that night, so we invited Nick to spend the night on our living room floor, since we live in a one bedroom apartment. It's been a year and Nick is doing so well. But don't think we are sacrificing! He cleans the house several times a week without me ever asking. He runs errands. He brings home bags of groceries, instinctively knowing what is needed. We've helped Nick get a job but he doesn't make enough money to get his own place yet, so we are looking into subsidized housing for him. We are helping him investigate community college programs and grants. And he is more appreciative than you can imagine.

I don't advise others to do this because you just don't know what you are getting. Nick says about 25 per cent of homeless people are more or less normal but that means 75 per cent aren't. Still, it has worked for us. People are always telling me what a saint I am but all I see is that we reached out in one small way to help one human being find some hope.

Heidi Eros, Photographer
New York

8 Love in Families

Perhaps the greatest social service that can
be rendered by anybody to the country
and to mankind is to bring up a family.
George Bernard Shaw

In recent decades the importance of love in families has been demonstrated by thousands of studies in social science, psychology and the newer field of brain-scan science. Attachment theory has received increasing attention and says that children who are loved and nurtured do better in school, have more stable friendships and relationships and are less prone to violence. Therefore the early experience of love in the family is the foundation of a virtuous and productive human being. In addition, adults who are married have better levels of mental and physical health, while couples who have higher skills in emotional intelligence, mindfulness or self-reflection have been shown to have happier marriages. Thus love helps children grow into well-adjusted adults and helps grown-ups have happier marriages.

Family is the foundation

> In the world of existence there are various bonds which unite human hearts . . . The first and foremost is the bond of family relationship . . .[1]

Love brings family unity

> If the members of a family are perfectly united it will add to their comfort and joy . . . 'Thy kingdom come, Thy will be done on earth as in heaven', will be a reality for each will have the kingdom within himself.[2]

> If love and agreement are manifest in a single family, that family will advance, become illumined and spiritual; but if enmity and hatred exist within it destruction and dispersion are inevitable.[3]

Brotherhood and sisterhood that is founded on a universal love is precious. It is not like the material kind which is soon forgotten and, perhaps, changed to hatred before this life is over . . . but this divine relationship is eternal. In the world of God it will become more clear and manifest.[4]

Nurture children

These children must be reared with infinite, loving care, and tenderly fostered in the embraces of mercy, so that they may taste the spiritual honey-sweetness of God's love; that they may become like unto candles shedding their beams across this darksome world . . .[5]

Respect parents

Comfort thy mother and endeavor to do what is conducive to the happiness of her heart.[6]

So you ought, in return for the love and kindness shown you by your father, to give to the poor for his sake, with greatest submission and humility implore pardon and remission of sins, and ask for the supreme mercy.[7]

Exercise

Think of the members of your immediate family: parents, siblings, spouse, children. Every family has positive qualities and ways it can improve. But just as Jonathan Haidt's research shows we are better off focusing on our strengths, we can do that in our families too. Complete the table on page 70, which asks you to list the positive qualities of your family and its members, as well as identify strategies and behaviors *you* can undertake to increase the well-being of your family.

Questions to ask yourself

1) What are the really great things about your family?

Positive qualities of the family

Family member	Positive qualities	How that quality affects others	What can you do to enhance the relationship?
1. Family in total			
2. Parent-mother			
3. Parent-father			
4. Sibling			
5. Sibling			
6. Sibling			
7. Spouse			
8. Child			
9. Child			
10. Child			
11. Other			
12. Other			

2) What qualities of the individuals do you cherish?

3) What can you do to make your family stronger?

Education of girls and boys

Economists, health researchers and social scientists have found positive out-comes when girls and women are more educated. Some of these include higher birth weight and lower infant mortality of babies, less poverty as women have more skills and can contribute to organizations, and greater well-being of families with a more competent wife/mother.

> Education holds an important place in the new order of things. The education of each child is compulsory. If there is not money enough in a family to educate both the girl and the boy the money must be dedicated to the girl's education, for she is the potential mother.[8]

> The girl's education is of more importance today than the boy's, for she is the mother of the future race. It is the duty of all to look after the children. Those without children should, if possible, make them-selves responsible for the education of a child.[9]

Preventing violence in families

> Ironically enough, the place where women and girls are most subject to violence and neglect is within their own homes, at the nerve center of the family. If families educate their daughters, and the commu-nity systematically encourages the education of girl children, both the family and the community benefit.[10]

> But the problem of violence cannot truly be resolved unless men are also educated to value women as equal partners. Any effort to protect

women against male aggression which does not involve the early training of boys will necessarily be short-lived.[11]

Boys and men must be given the opportunity to grasp, on the one hand, the harmful effects of attitudes and values which condone and even encourage violence, oppression, and war; and to see, on the other hand, the advantages to society, families and the girls themselves when girls are educated.[12]

Story: It's not about the cancer

One year ago came an abrupt awareness that very little of what the future held was in my control. This was not a small thing. Though I don't have an 'A' personality, I may have an 'A minus' one. In my life up to that point, I believed I had modified many of the hard edges I'd been born with. Working in groups enabled me to learn the art of cooperation, consultation and compromise. Being a mother and raising four children I learned to demonstrate compassion and kindness and be filled with a wrenching love that will inhabit me through-out eternity. I am also a daughter to an aging parent. This new relationship has provided me with ample opportunity to be conciliatory and forgiving and surprisingly objective when necessary. And lastly, a marriage, a unique combi-nation of him and me together for over 30 years, had 'rounded out my corners', as my brother-in-law once remarked. I have benefited from the giving and the taking. But most of all I have enjoyed the sharing.

I never expected to share anything that wasn't welcomed. We had been through the inevitable difficulties that come with every life, every marriage. All these challenges we weathered, together.

Then, my strong, healthy husband was diagnosed with the dreaded 'C' word. Definitely not welcomed. Not only does he have cancer but he was diag-nosed with a rare form of it at stage four – meaning it was all over his body.

Immediate shock gave way to action out of necessity. The attempt to con-trol any aspect of this thing that comes flying at you is like trying to catch water in a sieve. There is nothing to prepare you for this experience. You just have to learn as you go.

Every day is different based on ever-changing facts: adjusting to unpro-nounceable medical terminology and potions, medical professionals – learning who does what to whom and why, preparations and testing, symptoms, side effects; being in the hospital, out of the hospital, in the labs, out of the labs; meeting with doctors, doctors and more doctors. Research: Internet, friends, family, phone calls, support systems. Finding out the hard way what questions to ask. Needing to check and double check everyone. Trusting and wondering if trusting was wise. Found myself writing notes about everything and keeping a calendar as a lifeline. Discerning practical information and making decisions about insurance, finances, bills, who is going to take care of the dog, the Grandma, the house? Oh and prayer. We can't forget the ongoing prayer requests and mystical receipt of them.

Emotions run the gamut. Prayer is always a solace. Yet homework and footwork are absolute. On some days it's perseverance and patience that fulfills our part of this mysterious process. Other days it's picking up prescriptions and doing laundry. Whatever it is, we have to do our part. It keeps us focused and hope-filled.

We've been at this a while now, over a year, actually. He's not in remission yet but the disease has been reduced to two very stubborn locations. We have highs and lows like anyone. We aim to do only one thing each day. We have discovered that this is manageable no matter what, so we always complete our list for the day!

Because some meds energize him, we may accomplish more. We went to the river one day and he fly-fished while I read in the shade. He got all muddy and didn't catch a thing. We laughed about it. It was a good day.

Chemo is tough on the body. Sometimes it's a big deal even to get out of bed in the morning. So he'll drink a simple smoothie in bed followed by a clean toothbrush and a warm wash-cloth. Then we'll look at each other and smile knowing we're *both* suddenly too sleepy to get up yet. So we snuggle and snooze. That's a good day too.

My survival strategy for the past year wasn't a strategy at all. It's about who I have become as a result of this year's life lessons day by day. These daily tests have become as much a part of me as loving my children, serving others and breathing. My world is what God put before me, 30+ years ago and today. I am grateful for the man I married and the path we walk along together wherever it takes us. We go willingly.

After a while it dawned on us that this wasn't just about cancer; the cancer merely introduced us to the alternative reality of multitudes of people who suffer as a way of life. Suddenly, when you find yourself among them, they are no longer the exception, they become the rule you live by. Their comfort, their cure, their pillow, their desire, their joy, their rest, their nutrition, their spirit, their strength, their view of the world at that moment is what matters. His world is my world. His world has changed and I'm in it with him.

We bend to the task of the hour because we can, Sir.

Andi Seals, Artist
Nashville, Tennessee
April 2008

Dan Seals died 25 March 2009, surrounded by his loving family.

9 Hollywood Love

To be in love is merely to be in a state of perceptual anesthesia . . .
H. L. Mencken

I detest 'love lyrics'. I think one of the causes
of bad mental health in the United States
is that people have been raised on 'love lyrics'.
Frank Zappa

Set me as a seal upon thine heart . . . for love is strong as death . . .[1]

Almost any book on relationships by competent therapists or counselors, or any studies on relationships, show that long-lasting marriages are based on common values, solid communication skills, affection for one another and the ability to solve problems. Yet where do you find such qualities in popular music or in many Hollywood movies? Instead, what counts there is overly beautiful looks, a perfect figure, lots of money and high status, and these qualities become the calling cards for finding a mate. No wonder there are so many divorces.

Choosing

[The marriage partner] must, however, exercise the utmost care to become thoroughly acquainted with the character of the other, that the binding covenant between them may be a tie that will endure forever. Their purpose must be this: to become loving companions and comrades and at one with each other for time and eternity . . .[2]

[The potential partner] must take an interest in all the problems pertaining to thy life, and be thy companion and partner in every phase of thy existence . . .[3]

Before choosing a wife a man must think soberly and seriously that this girl will be his friend throughout all his life. It is not a temporary matter.[4]

A lasting bond and fortress

The greatest bond that will unite the hearts of man and wife is faithfulness and loyalty. Both must exercise toward each other the utmost faithfulness and loyalty and not let any trace of jealousy creep between them . . .[5]

Endeavor as far as you are able to lay the foundation of your love in the very center of your spiritual being, in the very heart of your consciousness, and do not let this foundation of love be shaken in the least.[6]

He . . . made [marriage] as a fortress for well-being and salvation . . .[7]

The Lord . . . hath made woman and man to abide with each other in the closest companionship, and to be even as a single soul. They are two helpmates, two intimate friends, who should be concerned about the welfare of each other.

If they live thus, they will pass through this world with perfect contentment, bliss, and peace of heart, and become the object of divine grace and favor in the Kingdom of heaven.[8]

Exert the greatest effort

You must irrigate continually the tree of your union with the water of love and affection, so that it may remain green and verdant throughout all seasons, producing the most luscious fruits for the healing of nations.[9]

Strive, then, to abide, heart and soul, with each other as two doves in the nest, for this is to be blessed in both worlds.[10]

. . . the two parties must become fully united both spiritually and physically, so that they may attain eternal union throughout all the worlds of God, and improve the spiritual life of each other.[11]

When relationship, union and concord exist between the two from a physical and spiritual standpoint, that is the real union . . . But if the union is merely from the physical point of view, unquestionably it is temporal and at the end separation is inevitable.[12]

Exercise

Think about your life partner. What qualities would that person have? Think also what the popular culture (movies, TV, songs) indicates would be the best qualities for your partner. Complete the table on page 78.

Questions to ask yourself

1)   What impact has the Hollywood myth had on you?

2)   What can you do to counteract that myth?

3)   Complete the questions below.

     a)   What places do you frequent where you might meet a potential life partner?

     b)   What hobbies and activities do you engage in where you could meet such a person?

     c)   What are the qualities of the people you meet at the above two places and activities?

     d)   Do the qualities in 'c' match the qualities you listed as your ideal?

     e)   Thinking about your ideal life partner and the qualities that person

Qualities of a potential partner

Popular culture says my ideal mate should have these qualities	What do spiritual writings say the qualities should be?	The qualities I should avoid in my life partner	The qualities I think I need for a happy, sustained relationship
1)			
2)			
3)			
4)			
5)			
6)			
7)			
8)			

would have, what kinds of places is that sort of person likely to frequent? What hobbies might such a person have? Where would this type of person hang out?

    f)   What can you do to increase your chances of meeting your ideal life partner?

Exercise

If you have found someone you might want to spend your life with, the better you know that person the less likely you are to have unpleasant surprises after you marry. You and your potential partner should answer the questions below, separately, and then come together to compare your answers. Circle AGREE or DISAGREE

1)   It is preferable for my mate to have equal or greater than my educational level.

AGREE / DISAGREE

2)   I expect to fully develop my career and for my spouse to support me emotionally and financially, if necessary.

AGREE / DISAGREE

3)   I think it is totally fine for me to be unemployed (and without children at home) while I 'find myself'.

AGREE / DISAGREE

4)   If I am not employed, I will do all the housework. If I am employed, we will work out a sharing arrangement.

AGREE / DISAGREE

5)   Husbands should do lots of housework, even if they work full-time.

AGREE / DISAGREE

6) There are other things to bring to a marriage besides money and housework.

AGREE / DISAGREE

7) It is preferable for the husband to make most of the financial arrange-
ments, regardless of how much money the wife earns.

AGREE / DISAGREE

8) We should pool all our money into the same accounts.

AGREE / DISAGREE

9) We should keep separate bank accounts. We should then each pay half of
all expenses, even if one person earns a lot more money.

AGREE / DISAGREE

10) Substitute mothers can do an excellent job.

AGREE / DISAGREE

11) Mothers with young children should stay home and care for them.

AGREE / DISAGREE

12) If there is a disagreement that cannot be resolved, the wife should more
often give in to the husband.

AGREE / DISAGREE

13) My partner should not gain weight and should always put a lot of time into
personal grooming.

AGREE / DISAGREE

14) It is more important for the wife to maintain a good weight than it is for the
husband. It is OK if he gains a little here and there.

AGREE / DISAGREE

15) I expect to go out in the evening with my friends and for my spouse to take
care of the children, if we have any.

AGREE / DISAGREE

16) If the husband gets a good job offer, making lots of money, the wife should be happy to move.

AGREE / DISAGREE

17) If the wife gets a good job offer, making lots of money, the husband should be happy to move.

AGREE / DISAGREE

18) One of us should put family first and one should put career first.

AGREE / DISAGREE

Questions to ask one another

1) What did you learn about the other person? About yourself?

2) Were there any surprises?

3) How did you resolve conflicts when they came up in this exercise? Did one person give in or did you keep talking until it was resolved?

Story: Commitment-phobe

I'd been a dater, uncommitted, rearing up and bucking off the latest girlfriend at the mention of anything about the future. I was never afraid of commitment. I just had never known anyone who could elicit the kind of raw passion that **is** that song 'Shameless', written by Billy Joel and sung by Garth Brooks. I heard it for the first time just after I'd met a girl named Elizabeth, who came from a very different life from mine. I had nothing in common with her close connection to her family, or her interest in small talk about the normal things that happen to people on any given day. There seemed no real possibility for anything lasting, so I kept her at the same distance I had the others. I was truly surprised when I found myself in conversations with her and was strangely enthralled by what I would have previously referred to as mundane.

Then I heard the song. The doors blew open; the walls came down and I suddenly could express the feelings that had been building. The song's uninhibited, completely open, yearning for intimacy changed my outlook. Some nine years later, as we tuck our 18 month old son in bed and relax after a normal day of feeding, wiping, corralling and cajoling, I don't forget the song. In fact, it's in the smallness of many moments that the song speaks to me all over again.

Travis Tyre, Editor
Dallas, Texas

Story: Finding true love

I met my husband 20 years after being divorced. First of all, let me say that I had to network like crazy to meet him.

When I was first divorced all I really knew about dating was what I learned from TV. I thought that if I were attractive, the men would be asking me out, and if the men weren't asking me out, I wasn't attractive. Girlfriend, don't wait for the men to ask you out!

At first I took little baby steps. I put a personal ad in the local arts newspaper that read: 'Harriet Vane in search of Peter Wimsey.' If you read Dorothy Sayers and you know me, you will say, 'That's perfect!' Otherwise you will say, 'That's a little obscure.'

Eventually, I was networking like mad. I would practically drag total strangers down in the street to ask if they knew any single men. That's how I met my husband, finally – through a friend with whom I networked. We were talking about business but we got around to our personal lives and she set me up with Tom.

Tom is a lovely man and we fell in love right away. I knew immediately what was going to happen. We met in February and for my birthday in October I requested a watercolor of the little house that was my sanctuary. I knew that we would be getting married and buying a new house. Tom, however, was clueless. In December he asked me if I wanted a set of All Clad pots. I wanted to say, 'Honey, you have a set, don't you know what's about to happen.' By the following May we had bought a house together and he had given me a ring. The hassle of combining two entire households into one, selling two houses and getting married was huge.

The thing that sustained us, though, was that we moved in together. Every day of waking up together is a gift. I adore Tom and I tell him that I will never, never take him for granted. I know that he feels the same way. We are grateful for each day.

Because we are adults, however, we know that romantic love is just a stage. Next comes real love. When we were planning our wedding, we decided not to write our vows because they would have been too shocking. I told Tom, 'We are promising to get up and try to love each other every day. But if you misbehave too much, I'm outta here.'

In fact, every healthy relationship is built from the same blocks. When the romantic love (chemicals) fade, I want someone who knows how to commit and I want someone who understands that love between adults (unlike love for your children) is not unconditional. Our children are astonished that we don't fight. I tell them that Tom and I know each other deeply and that you feel worse, not better, after you fight.

Nevertheless, there are places that we rub together. I am very neat to the point of obsessive compulsive disorder. Tom is casual, oblivious and untidy at times. I tell him, 'Tom, your clue that it's not time to go sit and watch TV is that I'm still in the kitchen working.' I remember that with the oblivious comes a sense of relaxation that I need to learn. Tom remembers that with the driven comes a tidy house.

I told Tom recently that he is the happily-ever-after ending to my story. He said that he is the happily-ever-after beginning. I tell my friends that God sent me Tom – and I'm not sure I even believe in God.

Barbara Moss, Attorney
Nashville, Tennessee

Story: Lost love

During the summer of 1967 I was about to be 17 and in love for the first time. His name was Peter and he was the same age. I was also completely enamored of the Beatles, entirely involved with their music, their charisma and their effect on my generation. They were what life was about: Carnaby Street, flower power, Beatles songs, love and Peter.

During that long summer of 1967, the Beatles' 'All You Need is Love' was top of the hit parade. It was our song and it was playing all the time everywhere we went. Love was what life was all about. Every time I hear that song I am filled with an intense feeling of joy and a very distinct and clear memory of how pure and incredibly happy my love for Peter was that summer. I love that memory and the emotions the song evokes for me. It never fades.

Peter was my younger sister's best friend's older brother. He was at boarding school in the early 60s and picked me out of a school photograph that his sister showed him. Of course, his sister thought it was hilarious that it was her best friend's older sister!

The first time we went out was on his parent's boat – *en famille*. Later that evening he rang me and asked me to go to the pictures. Of course I accepted. We went to see *Barefoot in the Park*. It was my first serious date.

After that we saw each other regularly, especially after we passed our driving tests and were allowed to use our mothers' cars. We were always together.

Our relationship always involved music and the 'theme of the time'. We went to lots of local dances and were involved with a huge network of local people. Give me a song from 1967 to 1971 and I can give you people, events and happenings associated with that moment. I suspect he can too.

But I wanted to go out into the world and have adventures. I broke off the engagement in 1972 and went to live in a flat in London's Portobello Road, which I loved doing. Peter was devastated (I now have a son who is very like Peter and I understand completely). He was involved in a serious car crash shortly after. I saw him a couple of times after that but we didn't maintain contact. I know that he has taken over his father's real estate business in southern England. I know I could find him and very much want to. Now we are both in our fifties there is so much to reconcile and share.

In retrospect (did you really want my life story? No one really knows how I feel about this), now that I have my own sons – and in particular one that has found his love at an early age (he's like very Peter and music is a big part of his era too) – I am sorry we didn't have the wherewithal to sustain this relationship. The last I knew of Peter was that he had married someone who likes to read Mills and Boon novels and that he wasn't very happy.

Barbara Bradbury
University of Auckland
New Zealand

Poem: How Many Roots 2
by Karen Sasani

How many roots to split a rock
How many threads to mend a frock
How many planks to build a bridge
How many rubs to smooth an edge

How many drops to etch a hole
How many passes to reach the goal
How many stops to make a start
How many tears to melt a heart
How many tries to make love grow
How many fears to overthrow

10 Love, Humility and Gratitude

Whoever undertakes to set himself up as a judge of
Truth and Knowledge is shipwrecked by
the laughter of the gods.
Albert Einstein

People who are grateful are happier. Lots of studies[1] have confirmed this, whether the study was about the positive effects of keeping 'gratitude journals' every night, or showing that those who keep gratitude lists are better at achieving their personal goals (including health and academic), or how grateful people have more optimism, vitality, life satisfaction and lower stress levels than others.[2] People feeling gratitude are less concerned with material goods, are less likely to judge others by the type and quantity of material possessions, don't feel as envious of wealthy people and are more likely to share their possessions.

Gratitude is quite distinct from a sense of indebtedness, which actually increases anger and stress. Interestingly, humility shows a positive relationship with gratitude, which means those with gratitude tend to be humble.[3] Further, humility helps inoculate people against their own inflated self-evaluations. Nobody likes people who are too proud, and it is not difficult to see such pride in someone else. But seeing it in ourselves isn't always easy. I've had times when I was unrealistically optimistic about my dreams, discounting friends' advice, only to be like Icarus who flew with waxed wings towards the sun until the wings melted. I got my comeuppance.

One way to stay humble is to focus on helping others or on developing our own virtues. What gets in the way of humility is ego, which mystical Judaism says covers our essence,[4] just as mud might cover a windshield. We can work to reduce ego's effect on us through learning detachment: removing our attachment to winning or being better, our attachment to being right and the need to have more than others, and our attachment to our accomplishments and achievements. Detachment is not having our identity tied up in such things.

Humility through loving others

But they who are wise shall be humble.[5]

By good deeds, pure lives, humility and meekness be a lesson for others.[6]

Cut out the love of self,
like an autumn lotus, with your hand.
Cherish the path of peace.[7]

Although they lift up the head of pride, show thou greater humility and meekness and treat them with the utmost submission and lowliness.[8]

He must seek after the comfort of all and with the utmost humility he must show forth kindness to every one.[9]

Grow in humility and meekness daily, until thou attainest eternal glory and everlasting grace.[10]

Therefore, under no circumstances whatsoever should we assume any attitude except that of gentleness and humility.[11]

The spiritual qualities acquired by the soul in the course of a lifetime – qualities such as knowledge, wisdom, humility, love and other virtues – are acquired gradually.[12]

Human society at present exerts a pernicious influence upon the soul of man. Instead of allowing him to live a life of service and sacrifice, it is highly competitive and teaches him to pride himself on his accomplishments. From early childhood he is trained to develop his ego and to seek to exalt himself above others, in the ultimate aim of achieving self-importance, success and power.[13]

Meekness not weakness

Weakening one's self physically does not necessarily contribute to spiritual progress. Humility, kindness, resignation, and all these spiritual attributes emanating from great physical strength are acceptable to God. That an enfeebled man cannot fight is not accounted a virtue. Were physical weakness a virtue the dead would be perfect, for they can do nothing.[14]

Detachment from the Kingdom of Names

The soul of man needs to be adorned with the virtues of humility and self-effacement so that it may become detached from the Kingdom of Names.[15]

For instance, generosity is an attribute of God, and it manifests itself in human beings. However, a person who has this attribute often becomes proud of it and loves to be referred to as generous. When his generosity is acknowledged by other people, he becomes happy, and when it is ignored, he is unhappy . . . Usually man ascribes these attributes to his own person rather than to God and employs them to boost his own ego. For instance, a learned man uses the attribute of knowledge to become famous and feels gratified and uplifted when his name is publicized far and wide. Or there is the individual whose heart leaps with feelings of pride and satisfaction when he hears his name mentioned and finds himself admired. These are examples of attachment to the Kingdom of Names.[16]

Exercise

To understand how the Kingdom of Names works for you, complete the sentences below and the table on page 89.

1) I am the kind of person who . . .

2) I was raised to . . .

3) I am known to always . . .

The Kingdom of Names

Qualities I have that I am proud of*	Good things other people tell me about this quality	How I feel when I get such feedback	How would my self-image change without this quality?

*such as generosity, intelligence, punctuality, humility, etc.

Questions to ask yourself

1) When you finished the sentences above, what patterns in your life did you see?

2) Which of the qualities you listed (in either the sentence completions or the table) do you feel most closely identified with?.

3) If you didn't have these qualities, what would your identity be? Who would be the real you?

Gratitude

Research shows that gratitude and other positive emotions help people become more resilient in the face of bereavement, deadly diseases and tragedy. Analyses of tests and difficulties show that even the most painful experiences often, later on, are much appreciated for their educational value and stimulus for growth. Gratitude also helps people create interpersonal resources that help to cope with adversity and stress.

Gratitude can be shown

To express his gratitude for the favors of God man must show forth praiseworthy actions.[17]

Be humble and submissive to God and chant the verses of thanksgiving at morn and eve . . .[18]

I yield Thee praise for all Thy goodly gifts and I render Thee thanksgiving for all Thy bounties.[19]

All that has been created is for man, who is at the apex of creation, and he must be thankful for the divine bestowals. All material things are for us, so that through our gratitude we may learn to understand life as a divine benefit.[20]

My gratitude to God knows no bounds.[21]

Now is the time for thee to give thanks to God with an expressive tongue . . .[22]

In this day, to thank God for His bounties consisteth in possessing a radiant heart, and a soul open to the promptings of the spirit. This is the essence of thanksgiving.[23]

The honor of man is through the attainment of the knowledge of God; his happiness is from the love of God; his joy is in the glad tidings of God; his greatness is dependent upon his servitude to God.[24]

Exercise

1) Choose two people who have done something meaningful for you but to whom you haven't expressed thanks. These could be friends, family, co-workers or even your high school English teacher.

2) Compose a letter of thanks to each person. Make it at least two pages long, if possible. Write in detail about what he or she did, what your reactions were at the time and the ultimate impact of his or her service to you. Praise them freely in the letters.

3) Ask someone close to you to read the letters, to give you ideas on how you can be ever more expressive in what you have written.

4) (Optional) Following the ideas of Martin Seligman in *Authentic Happiness*, laminate each letter.

5) If at all possible, visit each person and deliver the letter, waiting while he or she reads it, and then thanking him or her again afterwards.

6) Take notes (preferably in a journal or below) on how you felt writing, revising, laminating and delivering the letter.

7) How did this process affect you? What have you learned about yourself? About being grateful?

Exercise

1) Make a gratitude list:

I am grateful for:

    a)

    b)

    c)

    d)

    e)

    f)

g)

h)

i)

j)

k)

l)

m)

2) Buy a notebook and start a gratitude journal, something to fill in every night or every few days.

3) After having kept the gratitude journal for some days, answer the following questions:

   a) How do you feel when you list all the things to be grateful for?

   b) What is different about writing them down from just casually thinking about them now and then?

   c) Do you start to see the problems you have in a new light? How?

Story: Life's struggles and lessons

About 18 or 19 years ago when I was three months pregnant and my marriage was falling apart, my husband vowed up and down that there was no other woman. Right . . .

He played Kenny Rogers's 'Lady'[25] so much that I asked him to stop. It was virtually screaming at me because I knew in my bones that it was not about me, but someone else. Turns out it was about his soon-to-be second wife.

I had three sons in as many years, so my life was very busy and difficult. The last six months of this pregnancy I spent crying each day after I learned my husband of 10 years would be leaving me. He moved out when our baby (our youngest baby, because at the time they were all babies!) was five months old. The only way I could cope with this impending disaster was through denial. In my pained and twisted logic, I just KNEW that he was leaving me because I was getting fat again.

My sons' dad continued to play a part in their lives and my fabulous sons are now 19, 21 and 23. They have turned out to be gentle, caring, wonderful souls who enlighten the earth with their presence.

Recently I lost my job. A friend commented, 'You must have been DEVAS-TATED!'

I thought back to the time of the divorce and answered, 'No. I've BEEN devastated before . . . and THIS isn't IT.'

Through the years I've learned how strong and capable I am. But it was only after the divorce that I found my strength. I am truly grateful to God for giving me that test, the challenge that seemed so impossible and was so wrenching back then, because it made me who I am today.

Name withheld

Story: Seasons in the sun

My son, Philip, died at age 30 on the 5th of October 2000. About 13 months earlier he had been diagnosed with a brain tumour. He lived in Holland but was brought up on the island of Cyprus here in the Mediterranean. He and his wife (she married him when he was already ill and she was the truest of sweethearts) spent the last summer of his life here at home with his mum and dad.

It was a terribly emotional but also very rich time, and I am grateful for the closeness we could share those last months of his life. Sometimes I just had to leave the house so as not to let them know how sad and miserable I was feeling. I would just drive away onto some deserted roads and scream and cry. On one of those occasions a song came on the radio that I hadn't heard for many years. It was 'Seasons in the Sun'.[26] I had never paid much attention to it, thinking it quite soppy. Now it was as though my son was singing it. The lyrics were so close to our situation that every word sung went straight to my heart and soul: the 'Goodbye my friend' and 'it's hard to die, when all the birds are singing in the sky'.

The most poignant part was where the singer says goodbye to his papa, apologizing for being the 'black sheep of the family', recalling how his father had tried to teach him right from wrong. Philip had thought himself the black sheep of the family because he'd been rather difficult in his teens and although he and his dad had been friends again for years, something of the regret still lingered on. At that moment in time the words described what he and we were going through and I just sat and sobbed.

I don't think I can ever bear to hear the song again, it's so painful.

Marion Pnevmatikou
Cyprus

11 Suffering and Happiness

In the depth of winter, I finally learned
that within me there lay
an invincible summer.
Albert Camus

Tests can bring transformation

Kites rise highest against the wind, not with it. *Sir Winston Churchill*

What man actually needs is not a tensionless state but rather the striving and struggling for some goal worthy of him. What he needs is not the discharge of tension at any cost, but the call of a potential meaning waiting to be fulfilled by him. *Viktor Frankl*

Research on tests and suffering has shown[1] that adversity makes us stronger because it can help us develop resilience, which is a mighty force for our own growth and happiness.

Mary Lynn Pulley[2] undertook some of the earliest research in this field, interviewing people who had suffered the trauma of job loss several years previously. She found two types of responses. The first was bitterness and anger at the world. Not surprisingly, the lives of these people were now worse. In the other group, people were upbeat and had felt, even as they were getting laid off, that somehow the universe would provide for them. And they were right because they all got better jobs than they had before and also used this experience to examine their lives, to make them better. What distinguished these two groups was resilience.

Positive change through suffering is recognized by scientists, who have given it a name: post-traumatic growth.[3] Trauma survivors report better relationships, more appreciation for life, increased feelings of personal strength and spiritual development. They consistently say their losses have resulted in something of value.

These tests . . . do but cleanse the spotting of self from off the mirror of the heart . . .[4]

Thou art not shaken by any affliction or disturbed by any calamity. Not until man is tried doth the pure gold distinctly separate from the dross. Torment is the fire of test wherein the pure gold shineth resplendently and the impurity is burned and blackened.[5]

Men who suffer not, attain no perfection. The plant most pruned by the gardeners is that one which, when the summer comes, will have the most beautiful blossoms and the most abundant fruit.[6]

These afflictions are conducive to spiritual development and the descent of the Holy Spirit.[7]

The mind and spirit of man advance when he is tried by suffering. The more the ground is ploughed the better the seed will grow, the better the harvest will be. Just as the plough furrows the earth deeply, purifying it of weeds and thistles, so suffering and tribulation free man from the petty affairs of this worldly life until he arrives at a state of complete detachment. His attitude in this world will be that of divine happiness.[8]

If thy daily living become difficult, soon (God) thy Lord will bestow upon thee that which shall satisfy thee. Be patient in the time of affliction and trial, endure every difficulty and hardship with a dilated heart, attracted spirit and eloquent tongue in remembrance of the Merciful. Verily this is the life of satisfaction, the spiritual existence, heavenly repose, divine benediction and the celestial table! Soon the Lord will extenuate thy [straitened] circumstances even in this world.[9]

Be not grieved if the affairs are made difficult and troubles have waxed intense upon thee from all sides! Verily thy Lord changeth the hardships into facility, troubles into ease and afflictions into greatest composure. Verily, thy Lord is on the right path![10]

Suffering and patience

When you get into a tight place and everything goes against you, till it seems as though you could not hang on a minute longer, never give up then, for that is just the place and time that the tide will turn. *Harriet Beecher Stowe*

Behold, we count them happy which endure. Ye have heard of the patience of Job, and have seen the end of the Lord; that the Lord is very pitiful, and of tender mercy.[11]

Tests and trials shall soon arise, blessed are those who endure patiently! Blessed are those who keep firm! Be patient, that thou mayest be rendered victorious in thy greatest wishes, and know thou that verily, thou art with me in the nearness of my Lord, the Supreme.[12]

Take, my brethren, the prophets, who have spoken in the name of the Lord, for an example of suffering affliction, and of patience.[13]

Trials can bring happiness

Anybody can be happy in the state of comfort, ease, health, success, pleasure and joy; but if one will be happy and contented in the time of trouble, hardship and prevailing disease, it is the proof of nobility.[14]

My calamity is My providence, outwardly it is fire and vengeance, but inwardly it is light and mercy.[15]

Content with God's will . . . my heart surrendered . . . I was happy.[16]

Exercise

Think about some difficult situations you've had in your life, times that seemed horrible while you were going through them but afterwards you realized you had learned some important lessons. Complete the table on page 99.

Learning from tests

Briefly describe the test below	What did you learn from this test?	How are you a better person as a result?
1)		
2)		
3)		
4)		
5)		

Questions to answer

1) Is there a pattern to your tests? Does there seem to be a lesson you keep getting over and over? If so, why aren't you getting it?

2) What are the biggest lessons you've learned through tests and suffering? Could you have learned those lessons through happy times?

3) Which tests and sufferings are you most grateful for?

4) How is your life better because of your losses, your suffering?

5) Which tests were the most difficult? Did you grow more or less from those?

6) What were you like before you had all the tests above?

7) Do you agree with the saying 'What doesn't kill you makes you stronger'?

Suffering can bring blessings

There was once a lover who had sighed for long years in separation from his beloved, and wasted in the fire of remoteness . . . The doctors knew no cure for him, and companions avoided his company . . . Then one night he could live no more, and he went out of his house and made for the marketplace. On a sudden, a watchman followed after him . . . and barred every passage to the weary one. And the wretched one cried from his heart, and ran here and there, and moaned to himself: 'Surely this watchman is . . . my angel of death

. . . seeking to harm me' . . . Then he came to a garden wall, and with untold pain he scaled it, for it proved very high; and forgetting his life, he threw himself down to the garden.

And there he beheld his beloved with a lamp in her hand, searching for a ring she had lost . . . he drew a great breath and raised up his hands in prayer, crying: 'O God! Give Thou glory to the watchman . . . he was ... bringing life to this wretched one!'

Indeed, his words were true, for he had found many a secret justice in the seeming tyranny of the watchman . . .

Now if the lover could have looked ahead, he would have blessed the watchman at the start, and prayed on his behalf, and he would have seen that tyranny as justice; but since the end was veiled to him, he moaned and made his plaint in the beginning. Yet those who . . . see the end in the beginning, see peace in war and friendliness in anger.[17]

Tests are sometimes a mystery

It is strange how much suffering man has to put up with while on this earth. Our consolation should be however that it is part of a divine plan whose worth we cannot yet fathom . . .[18]

Suffering can bring joy and happiness

If you're going to be able to look back on something and laugh about it, you might as well laugh about it now. *Marie Osmond*

But and if ye suffer for righteousness' sake, happy are ye . . .[19]

Through suffering he will attain to an eternal happiness which nothing can take from him. The apostles of Christ suffered: they attained eternal happiness.[20]

I will no longer be sorrowful and grieved; I will be a happy and joyful being. O God! I will no longer be full of anxiety, nor will I let trouble harass me. I will not dwell on the unpleasant things of life.[21]

Be generous in your days of plenty, and be patient in the hour of loss. Adversity is followed by success and rejoicings follow woe.[22]

I know that thou art in difficulty, but this difficulty is conducive to the everlasting felicity and this weakness is followed by the supreme strength. Consider thou how the faithful women in the time of Christ, and after the departure of His Highness, underwent hardships! What difficulties did they not bear; and what calamities did they not endure! But adversity and trial, misfortune and derision, became the cause of imperishable and deathless glory and rest.[23]

Suffering brings growth

The more difficulties one sees in the world the more perfect one becomes. The more you plough and dig the ground the more fertile it becomes . . . The more you put the gold in the fire, the purer it becomes. The more you sharpen the steel by grinding the better it cuts. Therefore, the more sorrows one sees the more perfect one becomes.[24]

Do not grieve at the afflictions and calamities that have befallen thee. All calamities and afflictions have been created for man so that he may spurn this mortal world – a world to which he is much attached . . . Be patient and grateful. Turn thy face to the divine Kingdom and strive that thou mayest acquire merciful characteristics, mayest become illumined and acquire the attributes of the Kingdom and of the Lord . . .

This is the cause of the exaltation of man, the cause of his glory and of his salvation.[25]

The mind and spirit of man advance when he is tried by suffering . . . so suffering and tribulation free man from the petty affairs of this worldly life until he arrives at a state of complete detachment. His attitude in this world will be that of divine happiness. Man is, so to speak, unripe: the heat of the fire of suffering will mature him. Look back to the times past and you will find that the greatest men have suffered most.[26]

Suffering is both a reminder and a guide. It stimulates us to better adapt ourselves to our environmental conditions, and thus leads the way to self-improvement. In every suffering one can find a meaning and a wisdom. But it is not always easy to find the secret of that wisdom. It is sometimes only when all our suffering has passed that we become aware of its usefulness.[27]

Men who suffer not, attain no perfection.[28]

Trust in God

Rely upon God. Trust in Him. Praise Him, and call Him continually to mind. He verily turneth trouble into ease, and sorrow into solace, and toil into utter peace.[29]

If in these visible days and this present world matters appear from the realm of decree contrary to your wish, be ye not depressed, for happy and divine days shall come and spiritual worlds of holiness shall become manifest. In all those days and worlds, for you a portion is ordained, a sustenance is determined and a food is established.[30]

[Do not be] discouraged by any setbacks you may have. Life is a process of trials and testings, and these are – contrary to what we are prone to thinking – good for us, and give us stamina, and teach us to rely on God. Knowing He will help us, we can help ourselves more.[31]

Tests and trials only cause agitation to weak hearts. But the pure souls, a hundred thousand tests are but to them like mirage, imagination, shadow.[32]

Pray for strength. It will be given to you, no matter how difficult the conditions.[33]

Never lose thy trust in God. Be thou ever hopeful, for the bounties of God never cease to flow upon man.[34]

Exercise

Consider some situations you are now in that are annoying, perplexing or downright maddening. Is there a way you can turn them around to gain contentment, peace of mind and even happiness? Fill in the table on page 105.

Questions to ask

1) What are the things that most commonly upset you? Why?

2) What would you have to give up if you were to stop being upset at such things?

3) What is keeping you from changing to reduce your own unhappiness?

4) Do you want to be annoyed and angry all the time? If not, then when will you stop?

5) What advice would you give someone who was trying to be less angry and annoyed at others?

Take action

Effort is required:

> Success or failure, gain or loss, must, therefore, depend upon man's own exertions. The more he striveth, the greater will be his progress.[35]

> Man must be tireless in his effort. Once his effort is directed in the proper channel if he does not succeed today, he will succeed tomorrow. Effort in itself is one of the noblest traits of human character.

Turning annoying situations around

What is currently upsetting you?	What is it, exactly, about the situation that is upsetting?	Is there a way to change the situation or to see it differently? Describe.	What benefits can you get from making the change?	If you don't make the change, what is it that you are holding onto? What don't you want to let go?

Devotion to one's calling, effort in its speedy execution, simplicity of spirit and steadfastness through all the ups and downs, these are the hallmarks of success. A person characterized with these attributes will gather the fruits of his labors and will win the happiness of the kingdom.[36]

Five steps of prayer to resolve problems

First step: Pray and meditate about it. Use the prayers of the Manifestations [of God, e.g. Jesus, Muhammad, Krishna, Buddha, Moses, Zoroaster, the Báb and Bahá'u'lláh] as they have the greatest power. Then remain in the silence of contemplation for a few minutes.

Second step: Arrive at a decision and hold this. This decision is usually born during the contemplation. It may seem almost impossible of accomplishment but if it seems to be an answer to a prayer or a way of solving the problem, then immediately take the next step.

Third step: Have determination to carry the decision through. Many fail here. The decision, budding into determination, is blighted and instead becomes a wish or vague longing. When determination is born, immediately take the next step.

Fourth step: Have faith and confidence that the power will flow through you and the right way will appear, the door will open, the right thought, the right message, the right principle or the right book will be given you. Have confidence, and the right thing will come to your need. Then, as you rise from prayer, take at once the fifth step.

Fifth step: . . . Act. Act as though it had all been answered. Then act with tireless, ceaseless energy. And as you act, you, yourself, will become a magnet, which will attract more power to your being, until you become an unobstructed channel for Divine power to flow through you. Many pray but do not remain for the last half of the first step. Some who meditate arrive at a decision, but fail to hold it. Few have the determination to carry the decision through, still fewer have the confidence that the right thing will come to their need. But how many remember to act as though it had all been answered? How true are those words – 'Greater than the prayer is the spirit in which it is uttered' and greater than the way it is uttered is the spirit in which it is carried out. [37]

Exercise

Think of four or five problems or projects you've had in recent years. Choose some that you followed through on and some that you gave up. Fill in the table on page 108.

Questions to ask

1) What are the similarities between the projects you gave up on and those you continued? Did certain types of problems or projects wear you out more than others?

2) How did you feel about the projects you continued? Were you more satisfied or not?

3) What qualities inside yourself did you draw on so that you could continue the projects you did?

4) How can you choose projects more carefully in the future?

5) How can you get through difficult times better?

Story: Tammy saved me

Back in the year 1971 I found myself alone and expecting a child. The father was in Alabama and had beaten me so badly that I had to run home to my

Projects

Problem or project	Continued or gave up?	Was the decision to continue or give up the right one?	What would it have taken for you to complete the ones you gave up?
1)			
2)			
3)			
4)			
5)			
6)			

mother in Florida. I was only two months from delivery when I went to the hospital at 2 a.m. because my water broke. I told the nurses that I was scared, that something didn't feel right. They told me everything was fine and to relax. But this was my third child and I knew in my heart that something was wrong.

By the next evening, my son came. I asked the doctor why he didn't make any sound. The nurses kept telling me that some babies take longer than others to cry. I could see my son lying on a table to my right and the doctor using some kind of little paddle things on him. I could see him trying to give my baby mouth to mouth. Again I asked, 'Why doesn't my baby cry?'

The next thing I remember, I woke up in a strange room as a nurse gave me another shot and said, 'The doctor asked me to tell you that your child was stillborn.' Then I let out the loudest 'OH GOD!' anyone has ever heard.

It was hard to accept this reality – even after going to the funeral home and holding my son, or going through the motions at the funeral. I never spoke to anyone about what was in my mind or my heart. I bottled it all up inside.

Finally, I found a place to live on my own and I kept having nightmares about my son. I started getting drugs to sleep, drugs to wake up, drugs for the pain, booze to wash it all down with. I hated everyone and everything. My mom was terrified that I would commit suicide. I very nearly did several times. I would wake, start drinking, pop pills, drink more, pop more pills and so on until I passed out.

Back then we had the old eight-track tapes. I used to play them all the time, just for noise and company. Because at that time, no one wanted to be around me. I was sitting out in my car in the front yard one night, drunker than any sailor in any movie and listening to a Tammy Wynette tape. I had heard it many times but never truly listened. For some reason that night I actually heard it – I mean the words, not just the noise. Part of the song talks about the faces of loved ones who sadly place flower wreaths around a tiny grave and wonder why an innocent child has been taken when God could have prevented it. She thinks that God must have loved the child so much to want him sooner but knows that others don't understand the way He worked it out.[38]

That song, that night, was like a sledge hammer up the side my head. It was like a veil lifted from my eyes. It felt almost as if Tammy were singing to me, reaching out to me, telling me, 'There is a reason for everything, even if we don't know what it is or understand.' She got to me when no one else could. I went inside, poured out all the booze, flushed the pills away and slapped myself across the face HARD. Then I spent the rest of the night crying and begging

God to forgive my ignorance, lack of faith and the awful thoughts I had been carrying around inside me. I went to my mom and told her I would need some help. For the next few months it was back and forth, touch and go, but thanks to Tammy and that song I am alive today. If not for her and the idea that she was singing to me personally, I would not be on this earth. I truly believe that. She changed my life.

I am not going to sit here and say that my life turned out to be perfect or easy. It has been neither but at least I had a chance to live it. I can never repay her for what she unknowingly did for me. I just hope that up in heaven she knows that she saved one foolish girl's life.

Thank you from the bottom of my heart Tammy. Rest with God.

Robbie Keene
Clearwater, Florida

12 Love as Service; Loving Work

Happiness comes when your work and words
are of benefit to yourself and others.
Buddha

Turning love into a verb requires action. How can you show someone you love them? One way is to serve, to be as the servant. If you put yourself in the position of the servant, you must become humble, which is an easier place from which to love. Someone who feels superior and entitled will have more difficulty feeling or showing love. There are many opportunities to serve, no matter whether you are a mother, doctor, postal carrier, police officer, garbage collector, office worker or a neighbor. Everyone can do their job in the spirit of service to others, everyone can reach out and give a helping hand.

Become a servant

They must purify their sight, and look upon mankind as the leaves, blossoms and fruits of the tree of creation, and must always be thinking of doing good to someone, of love, consideration, affection and assistance to somebody.[1]

You live to do good and to bring happiness to others. Your greatest longing is to comfort those who mourn, to strengthen the weak, and to be the cause of hope to the despairing soul.[2]

Strive always that you may be united. Kindness and love in the path of service must be your means.[3]

Help me to be selfless at the heavenly entrance of Thy gate . . .[4]

Give me to drink from the chalice of selflessness . . .[5]

Service as the highest station; it is worship

Man's merit lieth in service and virtue and not in the pageantry of wealth and riches.[6]

This is worship: to serve mankind and to minister to the needs of the people. Service is prayer.[7]

Work done in the spirit of service is worship.[8]

That one indeed is a man who, today, dedicateth himself to the service of the entire human race.[9]

Let one live in love;
let one be adept in one's duties;
then joyfully one will see the end of sorrow.[10]

Make others' lives easier

I ask you not to think only of yourselves. Be kind to the strangers, whether come they from Turkey, Japan, Persia, Russia, China or any other country in the world.
   Help to make them feel at home; find out where they are staying, ask if you may render them any service; try to make their lives a little happier.[11]

If a man has done good, let him keep on doing it. Let him create an inclination to it. The accumulation of good means happiness.[12]

Jesus said, 'Love your brother like your soul, guard him like the pupil of your eye.'[13]

For, brethren, ye have been called unto liberty; only use not liberty for an occasion to the flesh, but by love serve one another.[14]

Exercise

Think of two people you either don't know as well as you might, or two people with whom you've had conflicts (or perhaps been annoyed with).

1) What one thing can you do for each person that will help him or her?

    a) Person 1:

    b) Person 2:

2) Write down *when* you will do these two tasks.

    a) Person 1:

    b) Person 2:

Serving a higher good

> Senses and faculties have been bestowed upon us, to be devoted to the service of the general good . . .[15]

> O God! Protect these children, graciously assist them to be educated and enable them to render service to the world of humanity.[16]

> Again, is there any deed in the world that would be nobler than service to the common good? Is there any greater blessing conceivable for a man, than that he should become the cause of the education, the development, the prosperity and honor of his fellow-creatures?[17]

Be ye a sprinkling of rain to every meadow and a water of life to every tree. Be ye as fragrant musk to every nostril and a soul-refreshing breeze to every invalid. Be ye salutary water to every thirsty one . . . an affectionate father or mother to every orphan, and, in the utmost joy and fragrance, a son or daughter to every one bent with age. Be ye a rich treasure to every indigent one; consider love and union as a delectable paradise, and count annoyance and hostility as the torment of hell-fire. Exert with your soul; seek no rest in body; supplicate and beseech with your heart . . .[18]

Wherefore, endeavor that with an illumined heart, a heavenly spirit, and a divine strength, and aided by His grace, ye may bestow God's bountiful gift upon the world . . . the gift of comfort and tranquillity for all mankind.[19]

. . . he that hath mercy on the poor, happy is he.[20]

Exercise

Doing something and getting thanked is a different experience from doing a good deed without letting anyone else know. Think of someone who isn't in your immediate family or closest circle of friends. What can you do for that person, something that would be truly appreciated? Do this service but don't let the person know who did it.

Questions to ask yourself

1) How was the 'secret' good deed different for you? Was it hard not to say anything?

2) How can doing good deeds without expecting gratitude help you to become detached from the 'Kingdom of Names', that is, the need to be seen as kind? In other words, what is it like to do something good without expect-

ing any kind of appreciation or gratitude but doing it merely because it is a good thing to do?

Work as a service

Hate not laborious work, neither husbandry, which the most High hath ordained.[21]

Work done in the spirit of service is the highest form of worship.[22]

Everyone should have some trade, or art or profession, be he rich or poor, and with this he must serve humanity. This service is acceptable as the highest form of worship.[23]

. . . the acquisition of sciences and the perfection of arts is considered as acts of worship. If a man engages with all his power in the acquisition of a science or in the perfection of an art, it is as if he has been worshiping God in the churches and temples.[24]

[Be] not slothful in business . . .[25]

. . . that ye walk worthy of the vocation wherewith ye are called.[26]

Studies in positive psychology show that people who are happy at work are more creative and productive, they make better decisions and work harmoniously with others. In short, the organization benefits from happy employees. Companies who want happy employees should note what it takes: interesting and challenging work, agreeable co-workers, decent supervision, fair compensation and benefits, and comfortable work space.

Exercise

Think of two places you've worked, the best and the worst. Fill out the table on page 116, which relates to these two workplaces.

Workplaces

Names of workplace 1) 2)	Best	Worst
What was your boss like?		
What kind of work did you do?		
What impact did your work have on others?		
What were the working conditions like?		
Was the pay/benefits fair or dismal?		
Describe your co-workers		

Questions to ask yourself

1) What patterns emerged from looking at your best and worst jobs?

2) Are there things you should avoid in your next job? How can you make sure you notice if those characteristics are there?

3) What conditions do you need to be really happy and satisfied in your work?

4) List questions you can ask to determine if a prospective workplace will fill your needs.

Story: Unexpected generosity

In 1989 I spent a year in Southeast Asia on a youth service project. It was an amazing year, filled with lessons, sacrifices, eye-opening experiences and so many examples of love. I was only 18 years old and it was my first real time away from my safe and small town in Orange County, California. At the time Cambodia was in the midst of a bloody war. I could hear the bombing and the cries of terror from my small hut, which was a stone's throw from the Cambodian border.

After a very full year in that area my time in Southeast Asia was coming to an end. I had to go back to the US but had grown so in love with this part of the world it was hard for me to leave. Five days before my flight back to the States I was walking to my little hut after a long day of teaching English to Cambodian refugees when I happened on a group of ten young people, aged between 12 and 20, playing soccer. When their ball was kicked in my direction, I kicked it back, giving them a friendly smile and speaking in my by then fluent Thai. I ended up talking to them for hours, and they invited me to play and eat with them, which turned out to be wonderful. They invited me to join them again the following week but I explained I was going back to the US.

As they all started talking, it was clear they assumed that I had to go back to the States because I had no more money to live in Thailand. So they quickly came up with a plan. One young man said that he had about $200 in savings (about two years' salary at that time) that he wanted to give to me to help keep me in Thailand. Another boy said they could have a community fund-raiser and a young girl offered her college fund.

I was blown away by this demonstration of love. At first I didn't know they were even talking about me. It was so strange to me. These people I had just met offering me their LIFE SAVINGS! And they were serious. I explained that I had to go back to the US and money was not the issue. After a very long goodbye we parted ways. But their generosity touched me so deeply because they expected nothing in return. It was out of pure, unconditional love that they offered their material possessions to a mere stranger. Funny how I went to serve, and yet one of the most profound experiences was the service I was given. I will never forget the love in their faces that day.

Mina Sabet-Bogan, Television Producer
Philadelphia, Pennsylvania

Story: East and west in one house

In 2001 we got a phone call from Rebequa Murphy asking us to sponsor an Ethiopian family whom she'd met and fallen in love with the previous year while on a visit to Africa. They had just won the US Green Card Lottery, meaning the whole family of two parents and five kids could emigrate to America, if they could find a sponsor family. The three oldest children had finished high school and two were almost done and they all wanted to go to college in the US. Because we were of the same faith, and also because Rebequa knew we always had a house full of people, she thought of us first.

At the time we had a young man named Glenn living with us, as well as two high school friends of our daughter Maggie, girls who had fallen out with their parents. What did sponsorship mean, we asked. Answer: They'd move in with you and you'd help them get jobs, learn the language, go to school and then get a place to live. Even though we had 7000 square feet, there were already six people living there. Add another seven and it starts to look like parts of India. Still, how could we say no? Within months, we found ourselves at the Rochester, New York airport, picking them up – in two vans.

As we drove home in the middle of winter, the children asked us why there were so many dead trees standing. We arrived home, and even though there were going to be 13 of us on three floors of 12 rooms, they were surprised that they would get four rooms, as they had fully expected all seven of them to live in one room.

We enrolled the younger ones in school, while the parents got jobs right away, housekeeping at a local hotel. Since neither of them could yet drive, nor could they afford a car, one of us got up every morning to drive them to their jobs at 4:30. We tried to teach them to take the bus but their English was so feeble, they kept getting lost. As time went on, one of the daughters got a job in a nursing home, which paid for her nursing school, and the older boys got jobs as well. One of the sons was deaf and had never been to school. He was placed in one of the best schools for the deaf, right in Rochester.

From the beginning they never let us lift a finger around the house. They did all the cooking and we'd have a contest to see who could get to the dishes first. All of them cleaned the house. At night we prayed together and enjoyed a lot of fellowship. In Ethiopia, they'd had an 'open house' like ours, so we fitted together perfectly. Our food bills were $2000 a month, the utility bills increased drastically, but within months they were earning enough to help out with those.

We taught them how to save money. Within a year they had bought their own modest house. And now, all of them are working, even the 12 year old. The oldest daughter married a doctor, two boys are enrolled in SUNY-Buffalo, soon to graduate in pre-med and pre-pharmacy, the mother works in a nursing home, while the father bought a cab and knows enough English to drive it and run his own business. We learned a lot of lessons from this:

1) 'Nothing is too much trouble when one loves, and there is always time.'[27]

2) Living together in harmony as we did requires similar values, comfort with lots of people in the house, high levels of integrity from everyone and a deep spiritual connection. The only fights we ever had were over who would do the dishes.

3) We established a pattern of serving one another, of doing whatever was needed. Consequently, we are always there for one another, even though they now live in their own house.

4) The bond we established has helped in solving personal problems. Their kids had some problems acclimating to the new culture or, more accurately, the problem was the kids adjusting but the parents not. We became the 'elders' in solving problems for them.

What seemed like it was going to be a sacrifice wasn't that at all. We found new people to love, people who've enriched our lives. We wouldn't trade our experience for anything, early-dawn job runs and all.

Bob and Debby Rosenfeld, Management Consultants
Rochester, New York

13 Become Love

*Love is that condition in which the
happiness of another person
is essential to your own.*
Robert Heinlein

*Your task is not to seek for love, but merely to
seek and find all the barriers within yourself
that you have built against it.*
Rumi

Happiness comes from practicing love, along with courage, justice, wisdom, knowledge and other virtues that have been written about over thousands of years in the various holy books. Psychologists such as Seligman and others have used science to demonstrate these truths. They also tell us that pursuit of pleasure and gratification do not bring bliss but instead can bring depression, which you might try to stave off with more material gratification, all of which ends in a negative cycle. Instead, choose love. Become love.

Be radiant in love

> . . . become so luminous that all your thoughts, words and actions will shine with the Spiritual Radiance dominating your souls . . .[1]

With love is heaven, without it hell

> Think ye of love and good fellowship as the delights of heaven, think ye of hostility and hatred as the torments of hell.[2]

> Love is the means of the most great happiness in both the material and spiritual worlds![3]

> We love to see you at all times consorting in amity and concord . . . and to inhale from your acts the fragrance of friendliness and unity, of loving-kindness and fellowship.[4]

Happiness is love

For material civilization is not adequate for the needs of mankind and cannot be the cause of its happiness. Material civilization is like the body and spiritual civilization is like the soul. Body without soul cannot live.[5]

Man is he who forgets his own interests for the sake of others. His own comfort he forfeits for the well-being of all . . . Such a man is the very manifestation of eternal happiness.[6]

Happy is the soul that seeks, in this brilliant era, heavenly teachings, and blessed is the heart which is stirred and attracted by the love of God.[7]

Strive with all thy powers in diffusing the spirit of real union among the people, so that all who are on earth become one family, loving, united, agreed, bound by the bonds of love and united with all harmony in all things and conditions; this is the greatest happiness of the human race . . .[8]

The happiness of man is in the fragrance of the love of God.[9]

Thank God thou art content with the will of God and art attached in heart to His divine wishes; and as thou art thus, all thy desires will be granted thee.[10]

Exercise

Think of two times in your life, one when you loved others and felt loved, and one where there was little love. Fill out the table on page 123.

Questions to ask yourself

1)   When you were unhappy, what material comforts did you have? Did they console you?

Love and happiness

Situation: describe it	What was your level of happiness/ unhappiness?	What lessons did you learn?
1) You had and gave love:		
2) There was little or no love:		

2)   What lessons did you learn about love and happiness?

We are made to love

> The obligation to obey the injunctions of Christ, to be kind, generous, forgiving, compassionate, devoid of prejudice or partiality, peaceable, is not something imposed by a ruler's decree or an external power; it proceeds from man's own nature.[11]

> . . . to love, to forgive, to create, to dare greatly, to overcome prejudice, to sacrifice for the common good and to discipline the impulses of animal instinct.[12]

Love is unlimited

> Love is unlimited, boundless, infinite! Material things are limited, circumscribed, finite. You cannot adequately express infinite love by limited means.[13]

> There is nothing greater or more blessed than the Love of God! It gives healing to the sick, balm to the wounded, joy and consolation to the whole world . . .[14]

> It is therefore evident that in the world of humanity the greatest king and sovereign is love.[15]

> What a power is love! It is the most wonderful, the greatest of all living powers.
> Love gives life to the lifeless. Love lights a flame in the heart that is cold. Love brings hope to the hopeless and gladdens the hearts of the sorrowful.[16]

Help me love

Create in me a pure heart, O my God, and renew a tranquil conscience within me, O my Hope! . . . Through the power of Thy transcendent might lift me up unto the heaven of Thy holiness . . . O
Thou Who art my God! Let Thine everlasting melodies breathe tranquillity on me, O my Companion . . .[17]

. . . confer upon me a thought which may change this world into a
rose-garden through the spiritual bounty.[18]

O Lord, enlighten my sight by beholding Thy lights in this dark night,
and make me happy by the wine of Thy love in this wonderful age![19]

Exercise

Complete the sentences below regarding love and blocks to love.

1) Last week, I had a hard time loving someone when . . .

2) It's difficult to love people who . . .

3) I feel so much love when . . .

4) It'd be so much easier to love, if only . . .

5) When I've tried hard to overcome resentments and prejudice, the result is
    . . .

6) The reason I hold on to some of my resentment is that . . .

7) When someone offends me, I usually . . .

8) When I offend someone, I usually . . .

9) The way I remind myself to choose love over anger, bitterness or defensiveness is . . .

Questions to ask yourself

1) Why is love a choice?

2) How many times a day do you choose love? How many times do you choose a negative emotion instead?

3) If you chose love more often, how would that help you 'become' love?

God teaches peace and love

> The Heavenly Books, the Bible, the Qur'án, and the other Holy Writings have been given by God as guides into the paths of Divine virtue, love, justice and peace.[20]

> He bids us worship in fearless loyalty to our own faith, but with ever stronger yearning after Union, Brotherhood, and Love; so turning ourselves in Spirit, and with our whole heart, that we may enter more into the mind of God, which is above class, above race, and beyond time.[21]

The divine purpose is that men should live in unity, concord and agreement and should love one another.[22]

My hope is that through the zeal and ardor of the pure of heart, the darkness of hatred and difference will be entirely abolished, and the light of love and unity shall shine; this world shall become a new world; things material shall become the mirror of the divine; human hearts shall meet and embrace each other; the whole world become as a man's native country and the different races be counted as one race.[23]

All the prophets have striven to make love manifest in the hearts of men. His Holiness Jesus Christ sought to create this love in the hearts. He suffered all difficulties and ordeals that perchance the human heart might become the fountain-source of love. Therefore we must strive with all our heart and soul that this love may take possession of us so that all humanity whether it be in the east or in the west may be connected through the bond of this divine affection; for we are all the waves of one sea; we have come into being through the same bestowal and are recipients from the same center. The lights of earth are all acceptable, but the center of effulgence is the sun and we must direct our gaze to the sun. God is the supreme center. The more we turn toward this center of light, the greater will be our capacity.[24]

Happiness from gender equality

The happiness of mankind will be realized when women and men coordinate and advance equally, for each is the complement and help-meet of the other.[25]

As long as women are prevented from attaining their highest possibilities, so long will men be unable to achieve the greatness which might be theirs.[26]

The world of humanity consists of two parts: male and female. Each is the complement of the other. Therefore, if one is defective, the other will necessarily be incomplete, and perfection cannot be attained . . .

Just as physical accomplishment is complete with two hands, so man and woman, the two parts of the social body, must be perfect. It is not natural that either should remain undeveloped; and until both are perfected, the happiness of the human world will not be realized.[27]

. . . there must be an equality of rights between men and women. Women shall receive an equal privilege of education. This will enable them to qualify and progress in all degrees of occupation and accomplishment. For the world of humanity possesses two wings: man and woman. If one wing remains incapable and defective, it will restrict the power of the other, and full flight will be impossible. Therefore, the completeness and perfection of the human world are dependent upon the equal development of these two wings.[28]

Questions

1) Why can happiness increase if there is gender equality?

2) Why does happiness decrease when there is no gender equality?

3) What are some ways that you can lovingly help to bring about gender equality?

Practice love

For this is the message that ye heard from the beginning, that we should love one another.[29]

Love thy friend, and be faithful unto him . . .[30]

He has cast away ill-will; he dwells with a heart free from ill-will; cherishing love and compassion toward all living beings, he cleanses his heart from ill-will.[31]

Do not only *say* that Unity, Love and Brotherhood are good; you must work for their realization.[32]

Let the love and light of the Kingdom radiate through you until all who look upon you shall be illumined by its reflection. Be as stars, brilliant and sparkling in the loftiness of their heavenly station.[33]

Be always kind to everyone and a refuge for those who are without shelter.
Be daughters to those who are older than you.
Be sisters to those who are of your own age.
Be mothers to those who are younger than yourselves.
Be nurses to the sick, treasurers for the poor, and supply heavenly food to the hungry.[34]

Be kind to all around and serve one another; love to be just and true in all your dealings; pray always and so live your life that sorrow cannot touch you.[35]

Enkindle with all your might in every meeting the light of the love of God, gladden and cheer every heart with the utmost loving-kindness, show forth your love to the strangers just as you show forth to your relations.[36]

Be kind to all peoples and nations, have love for all of them, exert yourselves to purify the hearts as much as you can, and bestow abundant effort in rejoicing the souls.[37]

Be ye a rich treasure to every indigent one; consider love and union as a delectable paradise, and count annoyance and hostility as the torment of hell-fire.[38]

It is incumbent upon everyone to show the utmost love, rectitude of conduct, straightforwardness and sincere kindliness unto all the peoples and kindreds of the world, be they friends or strangers. So intense must be the spirit of love and loving-kindness, that the stranger may find himself a friend, the enemy a true brother, no difference whatsoever existing between them.[39]

Therefore love humanity with all your heart and soul. If you meet a poor man, assist him; if you see the sick, heal him; reassure the affrighted one, render the cowardly noble and courageous, educate the ignorant, associate with the stranger. Emulate God. Consider how kindly, how lovingly He deals with all and follow His example. You must treat people in accordance with the divine precepts; in other words, treat them as kindly as God treats them, for this is the greatest attainment possible for the world of humanity.[40]

Why do we not love one another and live in unity?[41]

Make haste to love! Make haste to trust! Make haste to give! To guidance come!

Come ye for harmony! To behold the Star of Day! Come here for kindliness, for ease! Come here for amity and peace![42]

Turn all your thoughts toward bringing joy to hearts . . . Be the source of consolation to every sad one, assist every weak one, be helpful to every indigent one, care for every sick one, be the cause of glorification to every lowly one, and shelter those who are overshadowed with fear.

In brief, let each of you be as a lamp shining forth with the light of the virtues of the world of humanity. Be trustworthy . . .[43]

The wise, however, rejoice in giving
And thereby become happy hereafter.[44]

Do not be content with showing friendship in words alone, let your heart burn with loving kindness for all who may cross your path.[45]

Exercise

1) List six ways you can practice love during the coming week.

    a)

    b)

    c)

    d)

    e)

    f)

2) What other virtues do you need to be able to practice love in the situations you listed above?

3) How difficult will it be for you to complete this assignment?

4) Do you want to 'become' love enough to keep practicing at it?

> Love is the only force capable of transforming an enemy into a friend.
> *Martin Luther King, Jr.*

What is obtained by love is retained for all time. What is obtained by hatred proves a burden in reality for it increases hatred. *Mahatma Gandhi*

Story: Mobilize mankind

When we moved back to Oregon after living for five years in the Czech Republic, we yearned for more of that international service we had felt, a chance to use our skills to help people. So Gayle ventured to China in 2002 with the World Association for Children and Parents on a project funded by the Bill and Melinda Gates Foundation to build and start the first school in China for children with cerebral palsy. Because she is a physical therapist, this was a perfect assignment for her.

We discovered they had no equipment, no wheelchairs or anything for these kids, so we started finding used chairs and whatnot in North America that could be donated. But the project was plagued by too many difficulties and not much got done.

We decided we wanted to do something similar but closer to us and more accessible, both in language and by being able to drive there. Since Gayle speaks fluent Spanish, we both love Latin American people and Greg has a fondness for the desert and sea of Baja Mexico, we took an exploratory trip there later that year.

We contacted Amigos de los Niños (Friends of the Children), who said they did not work with orthopedics and referred us to a government clinic. We asked if there were kids we could help and if they could set it up. We took our evaluation forms with us to see the 25 kids they found and we spent the day measuring and taking histories. None of the kids had wheelchairs; they were all carried by their mothers – and some of them were quite heavy. We went back to Oregon, started a non-profit, 'Mobilize Mankind' and made the rounds, asking for equipment donations.

We took it all back in a trailer that had been donated to us by the Sunshine Lady Foundation. We distributed the equipment and had a party later that week. All the kids came back, in their chairs, with their parents and piñatas. For me, the high point of the week was giving seven year old Alondra a walker and braces. She had her mother carry her and the walker across town to the restaurant where her father worked. She wanted him to see her walk for the first time. The father was in tears. It was glorious – and captured in a photo. We got the idea of taking pictures of the kids using the equipment and sending them to the families who had donated it, so they could see the joy they had brought.

Within a year we had distributed 200 wheelchairs and were changing people's lives. By now, it's 500 chairs. Here were kids who had never attended school or who had been in a 'special education' school that had no way to deal with someone who wasn't mobile. For example, one place had a rule that you couldn't attend if you couldn't sit up on your own.

'What would we do with them if they can't sit up?' they asked us. We offered to get wheelchairs and they agreed to let the kids in.

Because we both want to do something sustainable, something that will last beyond our efforts, we are also working with the schools and therapists. Several times a year we bring down professionals from the US to give seminars to teachers and therapists on various aspects of physical disabilities, learning differences and education. Last year we realized we weren't having as great an impact on the administrators as we wanted, so we got five directors to come to Eugene and visit various schools to see what is possible. They went back to Mexico with so much enthusiasm about what can be done.

We work with the schools to mainstream the kids, now that they can move around. We've sent specialists to help the schools with curricula and we've educated therapists. One of our early challenges came from their belief that children with cerebral palsy should always lie flat, that if they sat up they'd get scoliosis. It took some time to convince them that seeing the world from the horizontal isn't a good way to live. We brought horse therapists down to train them in this new treatment. Our latest project is helping surfers get certified in working with kids with disabilities and they already have a project with children with spina bifida.

All of this has been done on sweat equity. We've received donations from individuals and larger ones from Los Cabos Children's Foundation but we work without pay, as we need the money to run the organization.

In many countries physically challenged kids have little access to recreation. We were tuned into this at a conference where a panel of wheelchaired young people explained that the one thing they missed from their childhoods was being able to hang out at playgrounds with their friends, to be on the swings, just to talk, to bond. When they went somewhere like that, as soon as the concrete ended, they had to stop and watch their friends from a distance. They all said it severely hindered their ability to develop long-term friendships. So we got funding from some governmental sources and rich business people in Baja to build an 80 per cent wheelchair-accessible playground, one that 'normal' kids will love too.

For us, this project has been the culmination of all the skills we've developed our whole lives. What a bounty to be able to use those talents in making lives better. On each trip we make to Mexico, there's at least one parent who breaks down in tears at seeing his child move on her own in a wheelchair. It means a lot to help unlock the burden these children live under in bodies that won't work as well as their minds. You never know what they are capable of until you give them the right equipment.

We will never forget Jose Arturo, a 12 year old boy who was so severely disabled all he could do was move his head. He couldn't talk or use his arms. The only school they'd let him attend was 'Life Skills', where they teach carpentry and laundry, neither of which he can do. We did some fund-raising and got a laptop and software programs for disabilities, getting it to work so that Jose could spell by tilting his head. The first thing he wrote was 'God Bless You!' Now we all see how smart and funny he is but before he was locked in a bummer body.

We feel blessed to be part of this project, that we have been given the opportunity to help these children. Funny thing about it, we are the happiest we have ever been in our lives. Materially we are really poor but we've got each other, fabulous people around us, work that is more fulfilling than you can imagine and a faith that gives us a connection to a higher purpose. What more could you ask for?

Gayle and Greg Edwards
Eugene, Oregon and La Paz, Mexico

Bibliography

General

'Abdu'l-Bahá. *Foundations of World Unity*. Wilmette, IL: Bahá'í Publishing Trust, 1945.
— *Paris Talks*. London: Bahá'í Publishing Trust, 1967.
— *The Promulgation of Universal Peace*. Wilmette, IL: Bahá'í Publishing Trust, 1982.
— *The Secret of Divine Civilization*. Wilmette, IL: Bahá'í Publishing Trust, 1990.
— *Selections from the Writings of 'Abdu'l-Bahá*. Haifa: Bahá'í World Centre, 1978.
— *Some Answered Questions*. Wilmette, IL: Bahá'í Publishing Trust, 1981.
— *Tablets of Abdul-Baha Abbas*. New York: Bahá'í Publishing Committee; vol. 1, 1930; vol. 2, 1940; vol. 3, 1930.

Abdul Baha on Divine Philosophy. Boston: The Tudor Press, 1918.

'Abdu'l-Bahá in London. London: Bahá'í Publishing Trust, 1982.

Albert, Deborah Fergen. *Embraced by Hope: The Resilience of Former Latino Gang Members*. Doctoral dissertation. Gonzaga University, 2007.

Appreciations of the Bahá'í Faith. Reprinted from *The Bahá'í World*, vol. 8. Wilmette, IL: Bahá'í Publishing Committee, 1941.

Argyris, Chris. *Overcoming Organizational Defenses*. Englewood Cliffs, NJ: Prentice Hall, 1990.

The Báb. *Selections from the Writings of the Báb*. Haifa: Bahá'í World Centre, 1976.

Bahá'í International Community. *Educating Girls and Women*. Statement to the 39th session of the United Nations Commission on the Status of Women. Item 2 of the provisional agenda: Priority Themes: Development: Promotion of literacy, education and training, including technological skills, New York, 9 March 1995, BIC Document no. 95-0309.
— *Ending Violence Against Women*. Statement to the 51st session of the UN Commission on Human Rights, Geneva, Switzerland, 1 February 1995, BIC Document no. 95-0201.
— *The Greatness Which Might Be Theirs: Religion as an Agent for Promoting the Advancement of Women at all Levels*. Introduction to the *The Greatness Which Might Be Theirs*, by Janet A. Khan. Beijing, China, 26 August 1995, BIC Document no. 95-0826.0.
— *Overcoming Corruption and Safeguarding Integrity in Public Institutions: A Bahá'í Perspective*. Presented at the intergovernmental Global Forum on Fighting Corruption II, The Hague, Netherlands, 28–31 May 2001, BIC Document no. 01-0528.

Bahá'í Prayers: A Selection of Prayers revealed by Bahá'u'lláh, the Báb and 'Abdu'l-Bahá. Wilmette, IL: Bahá'í Publishing Trust, 2002.

Bahai Scriptures: Selections from the Utterances of Baha'u'llah and 'Abdu'l-Baha. Ed. Horace Holley. New York: J. J. Little and Ives, 1928.

Bahá'í World Faith. Wilmette, IL: Bahá'í Publishing Trust, 2nd ed. 1976.

Bahá'u'lláh. *Epistle to the Son of the Wolf.* Wilmette, IL: Bahá'í Publishing Trust, 1988.
— *Gleanings from the Writings of Bahá'u'lláh*. Wilmette, IL: Bahá'í Publishing Trust, 1983.
— *The Hidden Words*. Wilmette, IL: Bahá'í Publishing Trust, 1990.
— *Prayers and Meditations*. Wilmette, IL: Bahá'í Publishing Trust, 1987.
— *The Proclamation of Bahá'u'lláh*. Haifa: Bahá'í World Centre, 1967.
— *The Seven Valleys and the Four Valleys*. Wilmette, IL: Bahá'í Publishing Trust, 1991.
— *Tablets of Bahá'u'lláh*. Wilmette, IL: Bahá'í Publishing Trust, 1988.

Balyuzi, H. M. *'Abdu'l-Bahá: The Centre of the Covenant of Bahá'u'lláh*. Oxford: George Ronald, 2nd ed. with minor corr. 1987.

Bhagavad Gita. Trans. Edwin Arnold, 1885. http://www.sacred-texts.com/hin/gita/index.htm and Ocean Research Library: Accessed at *Ocean* http://www.bahai-education.org/ocean/.

Bono, Giacomo, Robert A. Emmons and Michael E. McCullough. 'Gratitude in Practice and the Practice of Gratitude', in P. Alex Linley and Stephen Joseph (eds.). *Positive Psychology in Practice*. Hoboken, NJ: John Wiley, 2004, pp. 464–81.

Bostrom, Robert P., and Vikki Clawson. *Outcome-Directed Thinking: Questions that Turn Things Around*. Chicago, IL: Bostrom and Associates, 2003.

Buddha. *Dhammapada*. Trans. J. Richards. Ocean Research Library: Accessed at *Ocean* http://www.bahai-education.org/ocean/.
— 'Right Speech'. *Eightfold Path*. Ocean Research Library: Accessed at *Ocean* http://www. bahai-education.org/ocean/.

The Compilation of Compilations. Prepared by the Universal House of Justice 1963–1990. 2 vols. [Mona Vale, NSW]: Bahá'í Publications Australia, 1991.

Coopersmith, Nechemia, and Shraga Simmons (eds.). *Heaven on Earth: Down to Earth Jewish Spirituality*. Southfield, MI: Targum Press, 2002.

Csikszentmihalyi, Mihaly. *Flow: The Psychology of Optimal Experience*. New York: Harper Perennial, 1991.

Curtis, Anita. 'Thanks in Advance for Reading This Story: Psychologist Robert Emmons Explains Why Gratitude is the Best Approach to Life'. *The Ottawa Citizen*. 16 December 2007, B8.

Diener, Ed, and Martin E. P. Seligman. 'Beyond Money: Toward an Economy of Well-Being'. *Psychological Science in the Public Interest*, vol. 5, 2004, pp. 1–31.

Dunn, Elizabeth W. *Misunderstanding the Affective Consequences of Everyday Social Interactions: The Hidden Benefits of Putting One's Best Face Forward*. Doctoral dissertation, University of Virginia, 2004, AAT 3137289.
— Lara B. Aknin and Michael I. Norton. 'Spending Money on Others Promotes Happiness'. *Science*, vol. 319, no. 5870, 21 March 2008, p. 1687.
— Jeremy C. Biesanz, Lauren J. Human and Stephanie Finn. 'Understanding the Affective Consequences of Everyday Social Interactions: The Hidden Benefits of Putting One's Best Face Forward'. *Journal of Personality and Social Psychology*, vol. 92, no. 6, June 2007, p. 990.

Emmons, Robert. *Thanks! How the New Science of Gratitude Can Make you Happier.* Boston: Houghton-Mifflin, 2007.

Esslemont, J. E. *Bahá'u'lláh and the New Era*. London: Bahá'í Publishing Trust, 1974.

Exline, Julie, Roy Baumeister, Brad Bushman, Keith Campbell and Eli Finkel. 'Too Proud to Let Go: Narcisstic Entitlement as a Barrier to Forgiveness'. *Journal of Personality and Social Psychology*, 87(6), Dec. 2004, pp. 894–912.

Frankl, Viktor E. *Man's Search for Meaning: An Introduction to Logotherapy*. Boston: Beacon Press, 1963–2007.

Fromm, Erich. *The Art of Loving*. London: Harper Perennial, 2000.

Goleman, Daniel. *Emotional Intelligence*. New York: Bantam Books, 1995.

Graham, Pauline (ed.). *Mary Parker Follett: Prophet of Management: A Celebration of Writings from the 1920s*. Cambridge, MA: Harvard Business School Press, 1996.

Haidt, Jonathan. *The Happiness Hypothesis*. New York: Basic Books, 2006.

Harvey, Jerry B. *How Come Every Time I Get Stabbed in the Back My Fingerprints are on the Knife?: And Other Meditations on Management*. San Francisco, CA: Jossey-Bass, 1999.

Hendrix, Harville. *Getting the Love You Want*. New York: Holt Paperbacks, 2007.

The Holy Bible. Authorised King James Version. London: The Gideons' International, 1957.

Ives, Howard Colby. *Portals to Freedom*. Oxford: George Ronald, 1973.

Japan Will Turn Ablaze. Japan: Bahá'í Publishing Trust, 1974.

Kunzeman, Ute. 'Approaches to a Good Life: The Emotional-Motivational Side to Wisdom', in P. Alex Linley and Stephen Joseph (eds.). *Positive Psychology in Practice*. Hoboken, NJ: John Wiley, 2004, pp. 504–17.

Kurzius, Brian. *Fire and Gold: Benefiting from Life's Tests*. Oxford: George Ronald, 1995.

Lights of Guidance: A Bahá'í Reference File. Compiled by Helen Hornby. New Delhi: Bahá'í Publishing Trust, 2nd ed. 1988.

Lopez, Shane J., C. R. Snyder, Jeana L. Magyar-Moe, Lisa M. Ewards, Jennifer Teramoto Pedrotti, Kelly Janowski, Jerri L. Turner and Cindy Pressgrove. 'Strategies for Accentuating Hope', in P. Alex Linley and Stephen Joseph (eds.). *Positive Psychology in Practice.* Hoboken, NJ: John Wiley, 2004, pp. 388–404.

Manion, Jo. 'Does Your Job Make You Happy?' *The American Journal of Nursing*, vol. 108, no. 1, January 2008, p. 11.

Mansfield, Stephen L. *The Relationship of CEOs and Top Leadership Teams' Hope with their Organizational Followers' Job Satisfaction, Work Engagement, and Retention Intent.* Doctoral dissertation, Regent University, 2007.

Marcic, Dorothy. *Managing with the Wisdom of Love: Uncovering Virtue in People and Organizations.* San Francisco, CA: Jossey-Bass Business and Management Series, 1997.

Maslow, Abraham. *Motivation and Personality.* London: HarperCollins, 3rd ed. 1987.

Nabíl-i-A'zam. *The Dawn-Breakers: Nabíl's Narrative of the Early Days of the Bahá'í Revelation.* Wilmette, IL: Bahá'í Publishing Trust, 1970.

Nakhjavani, Bahiyyih. *Asking Questions: A Challenge to Fundamentalism.* Oxford: George Ronald, 1990.

New American Standard Bible. Various editions.

Olson-Madden, Jennifer Herold. *Correlates and Predictors of Life Satisfaction Among 18 to 35 Year-Olds: An Exploration of the 'Quarterlife Crisis' Phenomenon.* Doctoral dissertation, University of Denver, 2007.

Principles of Bahá'í Administration. London: Bahá'í Publishing Trust, 1976.

Pulley, Mary Lynn. *Losing Your Job, Reclaiming Your Soul.* San Francisco: Jossey-Bass Publishers, 1997.

Qur'án. Pickthall translation. Various editions.

Roethlisberger, F. J., and William J. Dickson. *Management and the Worker.* London: Routledge, 2003.

Salopek, Jennifer. 'Appreciative Inquiry at 20: Interviewing David Cooperrider', in *Training & Development*, vol. 60. no. 8, pp. 21–2.

Seligman, Martin. *Authentic Happiness: Using the New Positive Psychology to Realize Your Potential for Lasting Fulfillment.* New York: Free Press, 2002. www.authentichappiness.sas.upenn.edu

— *Learned Optimism: How to Change Your Mind and Your Life*. New York: Free Press, 1998.

Shoghi Effendi. *The Unfolding Destiny of the British Bahá'í Community: The Messages of the Guardian of the Bahá'í Faith to the Bahá'ís of the British Isles*. London: Bahá'í Publishing Trust, 1981.

Star of the West. rpt. Oxford: George Ronald, 1984.

Taherzadeh, Adib. *The Covenant of Bahá'u'lláh*. Oxford: George Ronald, 1992.
— *The Revelation of Bahá'u'lláh*, vol. 1. Oxford: George Ronald, 1974.
— *The Revelation of Bahá'u'lláh*, vol. 3. Oxford: George Ronald, 1983.
— *The Revelation of Bahá'u'lláh*, vol. 4. Oxford: George Ronald, 1987.

Tedeschi, Richard G., and Lawrence G. Calhoun. 'A Clinical Approach to Posttraumatic Growth', in P. Alex Linley and Stephen Joseph (eds.). *Positive Psychology in Practice*. Hoboken, NJ: John Wiley, 2004, pp. 405–19.

Townshend, George. *The Heart of the Gospel*. Oxford: George Ronald, 1972.

The Universal House of Justice. Letter written on behalf of the Universal House of Justice to an individual on the subjects of child abuse, psychology and knowledge of the self, 2 December 1985.
— Letter written on behalf of the Universal House of Justice to a National Spiritual Assembly, 16 February 1989.
— Letter written on behalf of the Universal House of Justice to an individual, including two compilations on scholarship dated 1979 and 1983, 13 December 1999.
— Letter to the World's Religious Leaders, April 2002.

Upanishads. F. Max Müller (ed.). Trans. various Oriental scholars. The Sacred Books of the East. Oxford: Oxford University Press, 1879–1910.

Vaill, Peter B. *Spirited Leading and Learning: Process Wisdom for a New Age*. San Francisco, CA: Jossey-Bass, 1998.

Wachs, Karen, and James V. Cordova. 'Mindful Relating: Exploring Mindfulness and Emotion Repertoires in Intimate Relationships'. *Journal of Martial and Family Therapy*, vol. 33, no. 4, October 2007, pp. 464–82.

Zell, Anne L. *Pride and Humility: Possible Mediators of the Motivating Effect of Praise*. Doctoral dissertation, Florida State University, 2007.

Music

Brel, Jacques. 'Le Moribond'. 1961. English version, Rod McKuen. 'Seasons in the Sun'. Recorded by Terry Jacks, 1974.

Chesnut, Jerry. 'The Wonders You Perform'. 1970. Recorded by Tammy Wynette, 1970.

Denver, John; Bill Danoff and Taffy Nivert. 'Take Me Home, Country Roads'. 1970. Recorded by John Denver, 1971.

Joel, Billy. 'Just the Way You Are'. Recorded by Billy Joel, 1977.
— 'Shameless'. Recorded by Billy Joel, 1989, and by Garth Brooks, 1991.

Lennon, John, and Paul McCartney. 'All You Need is Love'. Recorded by The Beatles, 1967.

Richie, Lionel. 'Lady'. Recorded by Kenny Rogers, 1980.

References

Introduction

1. 'Abdu'l-Bahá, in *Bahá'í Prayers*, p. 71.

1 Choose Love

1. Bahá'u'lláh, *Tablets*, p. 138.
2. I John 4:11.
3. Bahá'u'lláh, *Prayers and Meditations*, p. 248.
4. ibid.
5. Bahá'u'lláh, *Hidden Words*, Arabic no. 1.
6. ibid. Persian no. 3.
7. Proverbs 10:12.
8. 'Abdu'l-Bahá, *Foundations*, p. 99.
9. I John 4:8.
10. 'Abdu'l-Bahá, in *'Abdu'l-Bahá in London*, p. 53.
11. ibid. p. 79.
12. 'Twin-Verses', *Dhammapada*, vol. 2.
13. 'Abdu'l-Bahá, *Tablets*, vol. 3, p. 641.
14. 'Abdu'l-Bahá, *Paris Talks*, p. 179.
15. Matthew 19:19.
16. 'Abdu'l-Bahá, *Tablets*, vol. 3, p. 657.
17. 'Abdu'l-Bahá, *Promulgation*, p. 407.
18. Hebrews 13:1.
19. Buddha, 'Right Speech', *Eightfold Path*.
20. 'Abdu'l-Bahá, in *'Abdu'l-Bahá in London*, p. 83.
21. ibid. p. 122.
22. 'Abdu'l-Bahá, *Paris Talks*, p. 35.
23. John 13:34.
24. 'Abdu'l-Bahá, *Paris Talks*, p. 35.
25. ibid. p. 16.
26. *'Abdu'l-Bahá in London*, p. 72.
27. 'Abdu'l-Bahá, in ibid. pp. 75–6.
28. Bahá'u'lláh, *Epistle*, p. 14.
29. 'Abdu'l-Bahá, in *'Abdu'l-Bahá in London*, pp. 61–2.
30. 'Abdu'l-Bahá, *Paris Talks*, p. 30.
31. ibid. p. 29.
32. 'Abdu'l-Bahá, *Promulgation*, p. 337.
33. 'Abdu'l-Bahá, *Paris Talks*, p. 65.
34. ibid.

35. 'Abdu'l-Bahá, *Selections*, p. 88.
36. ibid. p. 256.
37. ibid.
38. Katha-Upanishad, First Adhyaya, First Valli, 27.
39. Taherzadeh, *Revelation of Bahá'u'lláh*, vol. 3, p. 35.
40. ibid. vol. 4, p. 193.
41. Bahá'u'lláh, *Hidden Words*, Persian no. 40.
42. 'Abdu'l-Bahá, in *'Abdu'l-Bahá in London*, p. 120.
43. From a letter written on behalf of Shoghi Effendi, 6 October 1954, in *Lights of Guidance*, p. 602, no. 2042.

2 Love and Happiness

1. See Diener and Seligman. 'Beyond Money: Toward an Economy of Well-Being', pp. 1–31; Seligman, *Authentic Happiness*; Manion, 'Does Your Job Make You Happy?', p. 11; Olson-Madden, *Correlates and Predictors of Life Satisfaction*.
2. Csikszentmihalyi, *Flow*.
3. 'Abdu'l-Bahá, *Paris Talks*, p. 29.
4. 'The Mendicant', *Dhammapada*, vol. 2, no. 25.
5. 'Abdu'l-Bahá, *Divine Philosophy*, p. 111.
6. 'The World', *Dhammapada*, vol. 1, no. 13.
7. 'Abdu'l-Bahá, *Tablets*, vol. 1, p. 51.
8. ibid. vol. 2, p. 270.
9. 'The Thousands', *Dhammapada*, vol. 1, no. 8.
10. 'Abdu'l-Bahá, *Paris Talks*, p. 175.
11. 'The Bhikkhu', *Dhammapada*, no. 25.
12. 'Abdu'l-Bahá, *Tablets*, vol. 3, p. 525.
13. ibid. pp. 673–4.
14. 'Abdu'l-Bahá, *Promulgation*, p. 204.
15. 'Abdu'l-Bahá, *Selections*, pp. 110–11.
16. 'Abdu'l-Bahá, quoted in Ives, *Portals to Freedom*, p. 52.
17. 'The Pairs', *Dhammapada*, vol. 1, no. 1.
18. 'Abdu'l-Bahá, *Selections*, pp. 256–7.
19. 'Abdu'l-Bahá, in *Bahá'í World Faith*, p. 356.
20. 'Abdu'l-Bahá, *Promulgation*, p. 24.
21. Bahá'u'lláh, *Gleanings*, p. 285.
22. 'Abdu'l-Bahá, *Divine Philosophy*, p. 54.
23. 'Abdu'l-Bahá, *Selections*, p. 72.
24. ibid.
25. 'Abdu'l-Bahá, *Promulgation*, p. 337.
26. 'Abdu'l-Bahá, in *'Abdu'l-Bahá in London*, p. 122.
27. 'The World', *Dhammapada*, vol. 1, no. 13.
28. Dunn, Aknin and Norton, 'Spending Money on Others Promotes Happiness', p. 1687.

29. Dunn, *Misunderstanding the Affective Consequences of Everyday Social Interactions.*
30. 'Abdu'l-Bahá, in *'Abdu'l-Bahá in London*, p. 48.
31. 'Abdu'l-Bahá, *Paris Talks*, pp. 109–10.
32. 'Abdu'l-Bahá, in *Bahá'í World Faith*, p. 217.
33. 'Abdu'l-Bahá, in ibid. p. 230.
34. Most happy to least: Amish, Inuit, college students, lottery winners.
35. Seligman, *Authentic Happiness*, and Goleman, *Emotional Intelligence.*

3 Trustworthiness, Wisdom and Speaking Kindly of Others

1. See also Kunzeman, 'Approaches to a Good Life', pp. 504–17.
2. Proverbs 3:13.
3. 'Abdu'l-Bahá, *Foundations*, p. 105.
4. 'Abdu'l-Bahá, *Some Answered Questions*, p. 47.
5. Bahá'u'lláh, *Tablets*, p. 57.
6. 'Abdu'l-Bahá, in *Bahá'í World Faith*, p. 218.
7. 'Abdu'l-Bahá, *Promulgation*, p. 149.
8. 'Abdu'l-Bahá, in *Bahá'í World Faith*, p. 356.
9. 'Abdu'l-Bahá, *Selections*, p. 26.
10. 'Pleasure', *Dhammapada*, vol. 2, no. 16.
11. 'Abdu'l-Bahá, *Paris Talks*, p. 65.
12. Bahá'u'lláh, *Hidden Words*, Persian no. 6.
13. 'The Twin-Verses', *Dhammapada*, vol. 2, no. 1.
14. 'Abdu'l-Bahá, *Promulgation*, p. 19.
15. 'Abdu'l-Bahá, *Secret*, p. 19.
16. Townshend, *Heart of the Gospel*, p. 31.
17. 'Anger', *Dhammapada*, vol. 2, no. 17.
18. 'Abdu'l-Bahá, *Divine Philosophy*, p. 99.
19. Bahá'u'lláh, *Hidden Words*, Arabic no. 2.
20. 'Abdu'l-Bahá, *Secret*, pp. 33–4.
21. Bahá'u'lláh, in *Compilation*, vol. 2, p. 334, no. 2037.
22. I Peter 3:10–11.
23. From a letter written on behalf of Shoghi Effendi to an individual, 12 May 1925, in *Compilation*, vol. 2, pp. 3–4, no. 1272.
24. 'Abdu'l-Bahá, quoted in Esslemont, *Bahá'u'lláh and the New Era*, p. 80.
25. From a Tablet of 'Abdu'l-Bahá to Dr M. G. Skinner, 12 August 1913, in *Lights of Guidance*, p. 91, no. 312.
26. Bahá'u'lláh, *Hidden Words*, Arabic no. 27.
27. 'Abdu'l-Bahá, *Promulgation*, p. 453.
28. 'The Twin-Verses', *Dhammapada*, vol. 2, no. 1.
29. Qur'án 26:83 (Pickthall translation).
30. 'The Holy One', *Dhammapada*, vol. 2, no. 26.
31. Bahá'u'lláh, in *Compilation*, vol. 1, p. 251, no. 575.
32. 'Abdu'l-Bahá, in *Bahá'í World Faith*, p. 266.

33. 'Abdu'l-Bahá. *Paris Talks*, p. 61.
34. 'The Fool', *Dhammapada*, vol. 2, no. 5.

4 Love and Forgiveness

1. Exline et al. 'Too Proud to Let Go'.
2. Ephesians 4:31–2.
3. 'Abdu'l-Bahá, in *Bahá'í World Faith*, pp. 250–1.
4. 'Abdu'l-Bahá, in ibid. p. 375.
5. Müller, Preface, *Upanishads*, vol. 1.
6. Student of the Just Governance Program, Nur University, quoted in Bahá'í International Community, *Overcoming Corruption*, 28–31 May 2001.
7. 'Abdu'l-Bahá, *Some Answered Questions*, p. 269.
8. Dowager Queen Marie of Romania, in *Appreciations of the Bahá'í Faith*, p. 10.
9. 'Abdu'l-Bahá, *Promulgation*, p. 453.
10. 'Abdu'l-Bahá, *Divine Philosophy*, pp. 41–2.
11. 'Abdu'l-Bahá, *Secret*, p. 95.
12. 'Abdu'l-Bahá, *Some Answered Questions*, p. 267.
13. Sirach 28:2.
14. From a letter written on behalf of the Universal House of Justice to a National Spiritual Assembly, 16 February 1989.
15. Esslemont, *Bahá'u'lláh and the New Era*, p. 22.
16. 'Abdu'l-Bahá, *Tablets*, vol. 2, p. 436.
17. 'Abdu'l-Bahá, *Promulgation*, p. 42.
18. 'Abdu'l-Bahá, *Will and Testament*, p. 19.
19. The Báb, *Selections*, p. 44.
20. 'Abdu'l-Bahá, in *Bahá'í World Faith*, p. 375.
21. 'Abdu'l-Bahá, *Paris Talks*, p. 154.
22. 'Abdu'l-Bahá, in *Bahá'í World Faith*, pp. 412–13.

5 Appreciating vs. Judging

1. See Haidt, *Happiness Hypothesis*.
2. See also Kunzeman, 'Approaches to a Good Life', pp. 504–17.
3. Bahá'u'lláh, *Hidden Words*, Arabic no. 5.
4. 'Abdu'l-Bahá, *Promulgation*, p. 93.
5. Hebrews 13:2.
6. From a letter written on behalf of Shoghi Effendi to an individual, 7 July 1944, in *Compilation*, vol. 2, pp. 12–13, no. 1299.
7. 'Abdu'l-Bahá, *Promulgation*, p. 397.
8. Romans 12:10.
9. 'Abdu'l-Bahá, *Promulgation*, p. 380.
10. Cooperrider, in Salopek, 'Interviewing David Cooperrider', pp. 21–2.
11. See Argyris, *Overcoming Organizational Defenses*.

12. Nakhjavani, *Asking Questions: A Challenge to Fundamentalism*.
13. From Bostrom and Clawson, *Outcome-Directed Thinking*.
14. Abdu'l-Bahá, *Promulgation*, p. 120.
15. 'Abdu'l-Bahá, *Selections*, p. 110.
16. 'Abdu'l-Bahá, in *Bahá'í World Faith*, p. 408.
17. 'Abdu'l-Bahá, *Divine Philosophy*, pp. 182–3.
18. 'Abdu'l-Bahá, *Promulgation*, p. 410.
19. ibid. p. 453.
20. 'Abdu'l-Bahá, *Divine Philosophy*, p. 106.
21. Bahá'u'lláh, *Gleanings*, p. 76.
22. ibid. p. 144.
23. Bahá'u'lláh, *Hidden Words*, Arabic no. 46.

6 Knowing and Loving Yourself

1. 'Abdu'l-Bahá, *Selections*, p. 150.
2. 'Abdu'l-Bahá, *Baha'i Scriptures*, p. 302.
3. Bahá'u'lláh, *Tablets*, p. 156.
4. *Bhagavad Gita* (Edwin Arnold translation), ch. 2.
5. From a letter written on behalf of Shoghi Effendi to an individual, 10 December 1947, in *Lights of Guidance*, p. 113, no. 386.
6. Bahá'u'lláh, *Gleanings*, p. 291.
7. From a letter written on behalf of Shoghi Effendi to an individual, 8 January 1949, in *Lights of Guidance*, p. 114, no. 388.
8. Taherzadeh, *Revelation of Bahá'u'lláh*, vol. 1, p. 77.
9. Bahá'í International Community, *Religion as Agent for Promoting Advancement of Women*, 26 August 1995.
10. 'Abdu'l-Bahá, in *'Abdu'l-Bahá in London*, p. 54.
11. Bahá'u'lláh, *Tablets*, p. 35.
12. 'Abdu'l-Bahá, *Some Answered Questions*, p. 188.
13. Bahá'u'lláh, *Gleanings*, p. 68.
14. Kunzeman, 'Approaches to a Good Life', pp. 504–17.
15. 'Abdu'l-Bahá, *Paris Talks*, p. 79.

7 Love, Hope and Transformation

1. Frankl, *Man's Search for Meaning*.
2. See Lopez, Snyder, Magyar-Moe, Edwards, Pedrotti, Janowski, Turner and Pressgrove, 'Strategies for Accentuating Hope', pp. 388–404.
3. See Mansfield, *The Relationship of CEO's and Top Leadership Teams' Hope*.
4. See Albert, *Embraced by Hope*.
5. Olson-Madden, *Correlates and Predictors of Life Satisfaction*.
6. 'Abdu'l-Bahá, *Selections*, p. 205.
7. Bahá'u'lláh, *Gleanings*, p. 323.

8. Bahá'u'lláh, *Prayers and Meditations*, p. 248.
9. ibid. p. 261.
10. 'Abdu'l-Bahá, *Paris Talks*, p. 112.
11. ibid. p. 179.
12. Haidt, *Happiness Hypothesis*.
13. ibid. p. 110.
14. Bahá'u'lláh, *Seven Valleys*, p. 35.
15. 'Abdu'l-Bahá, *Divine Philosophy*, p. 124.
16. Bahá'u'lláh, *Gleanings*, p. 328.
17. 'Abdu'l-Bahá, in *Bahá'í World Faith*, p. 386.
18. 'Abdu'l-Bahá, in ibid. p. 286.
19. *'Abdu'l-Bahá in London*, p. 72.

8 Love in Families

1. 'Abdu'l-Bahá, *Promulgation*, p. 320.
2. 'Abdu'l-Bahá, *Divine Philosophy*, p. 184.
3. 'Abdu'l-Bahá, in *Bahá'í World Faith*, p. 229.
4. 'Abdu'l-Bahá, *Divine Philosophy*, p. 112.
5. 'Abdu'l-Bahá, *Selections*, p. 21.
6. 'Abdu'l-Bahá, in *Bahá'í World Faith*, p. 361.
7. 'Abdu'l-Bahá, in ibid. p. 330.
8. 'Abdu'l-Bahá, *Divine Philosophy*, p. 83.
9. 'Abdu'l-Bahá, in *'Abdu'l-Bahá in London*, p. 91.
10. Bahá'í International Community, *Ending Violence Against Women*, 1 February 1995.
11. ibid.
12. Bahá'í International Community, *Educating Girls and Women*, 9 March 1995.

9 Hollywood Love

1. Song of Solomon 8:6.
2. 'Abdu'l-Bahá, *Selections*, p. 118.
3. From a talk given by 'Abdu'l-Bahá to Mírzá Ahmad Sohrab, 22 December 1918 (translated by Mírzá Ahmad Sohrab), in *Star of the West*, vol. 11, no. 1, p. 20.
4. ibid.
5. ibid.
6. ibid. p. 21.
7. Bahá'u'lláh, in *Bahá'í Prayers*, p. 118.
8. 'Abdu'l-Bahá, *Selections*, p. 122.
9. From a talk given by 'Abdu'l-Bahá to Mírzá Ahmad Sohrab, 22 December 1918 (translated by Mírzá Ahmad Sohrab), in *Star of the West*, vol. 11, no. 1, p. 20.
10. 'Abdu'l-Bahá, *Selections*, p. 122.
11. 'Abdu'l-Bahá, in *Bahá'í World Faith*, p. 372.
12. ibid. p. 373.

10 Love, Humility and Gratitude

1. Bono, Emmons and McCullough, 'Gratitude in Practice and the Practice of Gratitude', pp. 464–81; Curtis, 'Thanks in Advance for Reading this Story', p. B8.
2. Emmons, *Thanks! How the New Science of Gratitude Can Make You Happier*.
3. Zell, 'Pride and Humility'.
4. Coopersmith and Simmons, *Heaven on Earth*.
5. Enoch 5:8.
6. 'Abdu'l-Bahá, *Tablets*, vol. 1, p. 23.
7. 'The Path', *Dhammapada*, vol. 2, no. 20.
8. 'Abdu'l-Bahá, *Tablets*, vol. 1, p. 150.
9. ibid. vol. 2, p. 469.
10. ibid. vol. 3, p. 524.
11. 'Abdu'l-Bahá, *Promulgation*, p. 128.
12. Taherzadeh, *Covenant of Bahá'u'lláh*, p. 17.
13. ibid. p. 25.
14. 'Abdu'l-Bahá, *Divine Philosophy*, pp. 98–9.
15. Taherzadeh, *Covenant of Bahá'u'lláh*, p. 25.
16. ibid.
17. 'Abdu'l-Bahá, *Promulgation*, p. 236.
18. 'Abdu'l-Bahá, in *Bahá'í World Faith*, p. 359.
19. The Báb, *Selections*, p. 181.
20. 'Abdu'l-Bahá, in Esslemont, *Bahá'u'lláh and the New Era*, p. 99.
21. Quddús, quoted in Nabíl, *Dawn-Breakers*, p. 368.
22. 'Abdu'l-Bahá, *Tablets*, vol. 3, p. 529.
23. 'Abdu'l-Bahá, *Selections*, p. 179.
24. 'Abdu'l-Bahá, *Promulgation*, p. 335.
25. Written by Lionel Richie, recorded 1980.
26. Written by Jacques Brel ('Le Moribond'), English title and lyrics by Rod McKuen.

11 Suffering and Happiness

1. Haidt, *Happiness Hypothesis*.
2. Pulley, *Losing Your Job, Reclaiming Your Soul*.
3. Tedeschi and Calhoun, 'A Clinical Approach to Posttraumatic Growth', pp. 405–19.
4. 'Abdu'l-Bahá, *Selections*, p. 182.
5. ibid. pp. 120–1.
6. 'Abdu'l-Bahá, *Paris Talks*, p. 50.
7. 'Abdu'l-Bahá, *Tablets*, vol. 1, p. 223.
8. 'Abdu'l-Bahá, *Paris Talks*, p. 178.
9. 'Abdu'l-Bahá, *Tablets*, vol. 1, p. 98.
10. ibid. vol. 2, p. 311.
11. James 5:11.

12. 'Abdu'l-Bahá, *Tablets*, vol. 2, p. 311.
13. James 5:10.
14. 'Abdu'l-Bahá, in *Bahá'í World Faith*, p. 363.
15. Bahá'u'lláh, *Hidden Words*, Arabic no. 51.
16. 'Abdu'l-Bahá, *Selections*, p. 226.
17. Bahá'u'lláh, *Seven Valleys*, pp. 13–15.
18. From a letter written on behalf of Shoghi Effendi, 2 January 1932, in Shoghi Effendi, *Unfolding Destiny*, p. 429.
19. I Peter 3:14.
20. 'Abdu'l-Bahá, *Paris Talks*, p. 178.
21. 'Abdu'l-Bahá, in *Bahá'í Prayers*, pp. 174–5.
22. Bahá'u'lláh, *Tablets*, p. 138.
23. 'Abdu'l-Bahá, *Tablets*, vol. 2, pp. 264–5.
24. 'Abdu'l-Bahá, in a letter written on behalf of the Universal House of Justice to an individual, 23 October 1994.
25. 'Abdu'l-Bahá, *Selections*, p. 239.
26. 'Abdu'l-Bahá, *Paris Talks*, p. 178.
27. From a letter written on behalf of Shoghi Effendi to an individual, 29 May 1935, in *Unfolding Destiny*, p. 434.
28. 'Abdu'l-Bahá, *Paris Talks*, p. 51.
29. 'Abdu'l-Bahá, *Selections*, p. 178.
30. 'Abdu'l-Bahá, in *Baha'i Scriptures*, p. 224.
31. From a letter written on behalf of Shoghi Effendi to an individual, 23 December 1948, in Shoghi Effendi, *Unfolding Destiny*, p. 453.
32. 'Abdu'l-Bahá, *Tablets*, vol. 2, p. 251.
33. 'Abdu'l-Bahá, in *Compilation*, vol. 1, no. 308, p. 156.
34. 'Abdu'l-Bahá, *Selections*, p. 205.
35. Bahá'u'lláh, *Gleanings*, pp. 81–2.
36. Attributed to 'Abdu'l-Bahá, from the diary of Ahmad Sohrab, in *Star of the West*, vol. 8, no. 1, p. 21.
37. Attributed to Shoghi Effendi. Excerpted from the pilgrims' notes of Ruth Moffat, an early American Bahá'í, in *Principles of Bahá'í Administration*, pp. 90–1.
38. 'The Wonders You Perform', written by Jerry Chesnut, 1970, sung by Tammy Wynette.

12 Love as Service; Loving Work

1. 'Abdu'l-Bahá, in *Bahá'í World Faith*, p. 215.
2. 'Abdu'l-Bahá, *Paris Talks*, pp. 112–13.
3. 'Abdu'l-Bahá, in *'Abdu'l-Bahá in London*, p. 122.
4. 'Abdu'l-Bahá, *Selections*, pp. 319–20.
5. ibid. pp. 320.
6. Bahá'u'lláh, *Tablets*, p. 138.
7. 'Abdu'l-Bahá, *Paris Talks*, p. 177.

8. 'Abdu'l-Bahá in *Baha'i Scriptures*, p. 278.
9. Bahá'u'lláh, *Tablets*, p. 167.
10. 'The Mendicant', *Dhammapada*, vol. 2, no. 25.
11. 'Abdu'l-Bahá, *Paris Talks*, p. 15.
12. 'Evil', *Dhammapada*, vol. 1, no. 9.
13. Thomas 2:25.
14. Galatians 5:13.
15. 'Abdu'l-Bahá, *Secret*, p. 3.
16. 'Abdu'l-Bahá, in *Bahá'í Prayers*, p. 28.
17. 'Abdu'l-Bahá, *Secret*, p. 103.
18. 'Abdu'l-Bahá, in *Bahá'í World Faith*, p. 356.
19. Esslemont, *Bahá'u'lláh and the New Era*, p. 226.
20. Proverbs 14:21.
21. Sirach 7:15.
22. 'Abdu'l-Bahá, in *Compilation*, p. 313, no. 704.
23. 'Abdu'l-Bahá, in *'Abdu'l-Bahá in London*, p. 93.
24. 'Abdu'l-Bahá, in *Bahá'í World Faith*, pp. 377–8.
25. Romans 12:11.
26. Ephesians 4:1.
27. 'Abdu'l-Bahá, in Ives, *Portals to Freedom*, p. 52.

13 Become Love

1. 'Abdu'l-Bahá, *Paris Talks*, p. 98.
2. 'Abdu'l-Bahá, *Selections*, p. 245.
3. 'Abdu'l-Bahá, *Tablets*, vol. 3, p. 525.
4. Bahá'u'lláh, *Gleanings*, p. 315.
5. 'Abdu'l-Bahá, in *'Abdu'l-Bahá in London*, p. 30.
6. 'Abdu'l-Bahá, *Foundations*, p. 42.
7. From a letter of 'Abdu'l-Bahá to an individual, 27 December 1918, in *Japan Will Turn Ablaze*, p. 23.
8. 'Abdu'l-Bahá, *Tablets*, vol. 1, p. 57.
9. 'Abdu'l-Bahá, *Promulgation*, p. 185.
10. 'Abdu'l-Bahá, *Tablets*, vol. 2, p. 456.
11. Townshend, *Heart of the Gospel*, p. 29.
12. The Universal House of Justice, Letter to the World's Religious Leaders, April 2002, para. 14.
13. 'Abdu'l-Bahá, *Paris Talks*, p. 36.
14. ibid. p. 82.
15. 'Abdu'l-Bahá, *Foundations*, p. 88.
16. 'Abdu'l-Bahá, *Paris Talks*, p. 179.
17. Bahá'u'lláh, *Prayers and Meditations*, p. 248.
18. 'Abdu'l-Bahá, *Tablets*, vol. 3, p. 641.
19. ibid. pp. 676–7.

20. 'Abdu'l-Bahá, *Paris Talks*, pp. 61–2.

21. Professor Michael Sadler, in *'Abdu'l-Bahá in London*, p. 34.

22. 'Abdu'l-Bahá, in *Bahá'í World Faith*, p. 245.

23. 'Abdu'l-Bahá, *'Abdu'l-Bahá in London*, p. 38.

24. 'Abdu'l-Bahá, in *Bahá'í World Faith*, pp. 218–19.

25. 'Abdu'l-Bahá, in ibid. p. 241.

26. 'Abdu'l-Bahá, *Paris Talks*, p. 133.

27. 'Abdu'l-Bahá, *Promulgation*, p. 134.

28. ibid. p. 318.

29. I John 3:11.

30. Sirach 27:17.

31. Buddha, 'Absence of the Five Hindrances', *Eightfold Path*.

32. 'Abdu'l-Bahá, in *'Abdu'l-Bahá in London*, p. 60.

33. 'Abdu'l-Bahá, *Promulgation*, p. 8.

34. 'Abdu'l-Bahá, in *Abdu'l-Bahá in London*, pp. 75–6.

35. ibid. p. 83.

36. 'Abdu'l-Bahá, in *Bahá'í World Faith*, p. 353.

37. ibid. p. 356.

38. ibid.

39. ibid. p. 445.

40. 'Abdu'l-Bahá, *Foundations*, p. 73.

41. 'Abdu'l-Bahá, *Paris Talks*, p. 120.

42. 'Abdu'l-Bahá, *Selections*, p. 273.

43. 'Abdu'l-Bahá, *Promulgation*, p. 453.

44. 'The World', *Dhammapada*, vol. 3, no. 13.

45. 'Abdu'l-Bahá, *Paris Talks* p. 15.